A Comparative Analysis of the Impact of Healthcare Insurance Availability on Health Outcomes in Hawai'i and Mississippi

James G. Lenhart, MD, FAAFP, MPH

SLEEPING GIANT

Sleeping Giant Publishing, LLC
www.sleepinggiantpublishing.com

MPH Dissertation

The University of Liverpool/Laureate MPH Program
James G. Lenhart, MD, FAAFP, MPH

An Analysis of the Impact of Healthcare Insurance Availability on Health Outcomes in Hawai'i and Mississippi

Submitted as partial fulfillment of the Requirements for the Degree

Master of Public Health

March 28, 2010

Copyright © 2012 by James Lenhart

First Edition printing 2012

Manufactured and printed in the United States of America

To learn about the author visit him at
jameslenhart.net

1. Medical – Public Health. 2. Medical – Health Policy. 3. Social Science – Disease & Health Issues.

ISBN: 978-0-983-52772-5
Library of Congress Cataloging-in-Publication Data

BE HEALTHY! BE HAPPY!

MPH Dissertation

The University of Liverpool/Laureate MPH Program
James G. Lenhart, MD, FAAFP, MPH

An Analysis of the Impact of Healthcare Insurance Availability on Health Outcomes in Hawai'i and Mississippi

Submitted as partial fulfillment of the Requirements for the Degree

Master of Public Health

March 28, 2010

DECLARATION

No portion of this work has been submitted in support of an application for degree or qualification of this or any other University or institute of learning.

James G. Lenhart, M.D.
Signature

ABSTRACT

Background and Objectives: Several studies have demonstrated the impact of health insurance prevalence on healthcare access and the impact of healthcare access on health outcomes. This investigation compared, contrasted and analyzed the impact of healthcare insurance availability on health outcomes in Hawai'i and Mississippi to test the hypothesis that health insurance prevalence improves access to care and health outcomes. It aimed to recommend public policy that improves healthcare insurance prevalence in the U.S. as well as public policy that improves health insurance plan characteristics.

Methods: This study analyzed secondary data extracted from the 2007 Behavioral Risk Factor Surveillance System (BRFSS) survey for the states of Hawai'i and Mississippi. Self-reported BRFSS data from the states of Hawai'i and Mississippi on persons aged 19 through 64 were downloaded directly into SPSS from the CDC and analyzed. Variables of interest like health insurance status and delay in care due to costs were subjected to bivariate and multivariate logistic regression analysis.

Results: In the 2007 BRFSS survey 92.9% (95% CI 91.7% - 93.7%) of Hawai'ians had health insurance; whereas in Mississippi 77.1% (95% CI 75.3% - 78.7%) had health insurance. This was significant at $p < 0.001$. Multivariate regression analysis supported the hypothesis that the increased prevalence of health insurance in Hawai'i improved access to care in Hawai'i to a greater degree than Mississippi. It was significantly less necessary for Hawai'ians ($p < 0.000036$) to delay care because of costs than residents of Mississippi – odds ratios Hawai'i 8.093 (95% CI 5.237 - 12.507) and Mississippi 3.221 (95% CI 2.489 - 4.168).

Conclusions: Health insurance status impacts access to care and health outcomes. U.S. states and the United States should adopt public policy that improves health insurance prevalence and insurance plan coverage for essential health services.

Abstract word count: 295

Key search terms: health insurance, health outcomes, delay in healthcare due to costs, BRFSS, United Health Foundation, The Commonwealth Fund, the Kaiser Family Foundation, Medicaid

Dissertation word count: 10,998

ACKNOWLEDGEMENTS

I wish to acknowledge and thank the following individuals who provided the guidance and inspiration necessary to bring this dissertation to fruition:

Jill Wiseberg – Dissertation Advisor for her advice and patience in providing guidance in the quantitative analysis, the dynamics of dissertations and document construction.

Jackie Wilson – Laureate Online student manager for her support throughout my MPH studies and this dissertation.

Kathy Finn – medical transcriptionist for her assistance in manuscript preparation.

Taylor Moseley – data analyst for his direction and support in bringing the data to accurate and meaningful conclusion.

Nancy Lenhart – my very best friend and loving wife who inspired me every day during the entire course of MPH study *and* who sacrificed countless hours of spending fun time together, not to mention the financial resource to pay the costs of my continuing medical education.

LIST OF ABBREVIATIONS

AHR – America's Health Rankings

BRFSS – Behavioral Risk Surveillance System

CATI – Computer-Assisted Telephone Interview

CDC – Centers for Disease Control and Prevention

CF – The Commonwealth Fund

CI – Confidence Interval

CMS – Centers for Medicare and Medicaid Services

EBSA – Employees Benefits Security Administration

Fed – The U.S. Federal Government

FPL – Federal Poverty Level

HALE – Healthy life expectancy

HDCCA – Hawai'i Department of Commerce and Consumer Affairs

HDLIR – Hawai'i Department of Labor and Industrial Relations

HI – Hawai'i

HMO – Health Maintenance Organization

KFF – Kaiser Family Foundation

MID – Mississippi Insurance Department

MS – Mississippi

MSDH - The Mississippi State Department of Health

MVLR – Multivariate Logistic Regression

NAIC – National Association of Insurance Commissioners

NHIS – National Health Interview Survey

OR – Odds Ratio

PEBP – Public Employees Benefit Programs

PHC – Prepaid Health Care Act

SPSS – Statistical Package for the Social Sciences

SUDAAN – Survey Data Analysis

U.S. – United States

UHF – United Health Foundation

WHO – World Health Organization

YPLL-75 – years of potential life lost due to death before age 75 years

GLOSSARY of TERMS

AHR – *America's Health Rankings* an annual analysis of health outcomes in the U.S. published by the United Health Foundation.

BRFSS – Behavioral Risk Surveillance System a U.S. wide telephone survey conducted annually by the Centers for Disease Control and Prevention that tracts self-reported health outcomes data.

CDC – Centers for Disease Control and Prevention a branch of the United States Department of Health and Human Services dedicated to health promotion and disease prevention.

CF – The Commonwealth Fund a private not for profit U.S. foundation that advocates for high performing healthcare and healthcare systems.

FPL – Federal Poverty Level poverty guidelines issued each year by the Department of Health and Human Services. The guidelines are a simplification of poverty thresholds for use for administrative purposes — for instance, determining financial eligibility for certain federal programs.

HALE – healthy life expectancy is the average number of years that a person can expect to live in "full health" by taking into account years lived in less than full health due to disease and/or injury.

KFF – Kaiser Family Foundation is leader in health policy and communications in the U.S. The Kaiser Family Foundation is a non-profit, private operating foundation focusing on the major health care issues facing the U.S., as well as the U.S. role in global health policy. Unlike grant-making foundations, Kaiser develops and runs its own research and communications programs, sometimes in partnership with other non-profit research organizations or major media companies.

PEBP – The Public Employees' Benefits Programs provide healthcare and retirement solutions for employees of federal, state, county and city governmental entities.

PHC – Prepaid Health Care Act originally enacted in 1974, the Hawai'i PHC Act was the first in the nation to set minimum standards of health care benefits for workers.

SPSS – Statistical Package for the Social Sciences is a powerful software application that permits analysis and interpretation of almost any data including social science data. SPSS was utilized for data analysis in this treatise.

SUDAAN – Survey Data Analysis, according to the developer SUDAAN is an internationally recognized statistical software package that specializes in providing efficient and accurate analysis of data from complex studies. SUDAAN is ideal for the proper analysis of data from surveys and experimental studies. SUDAAN was not used for analysis in this treatise.

UHF – United Health Foundation works to improve the quality and cost effectiveness of medical outcomes, expand access to health care services and enhance the well being of communities.

YPLL-75 – years of potential life lost due to death before age 75 years.

TABLE of CONTENTS
for
An Analysis of the Impact of Healthcare Insurance Availability on Health Outcomes in Hawai'i and Mississippi

TABLE OF CONTENTS
for
An Analysis of the Impact of Healthcare Insurance Availability on Health Outcomes in Hawai'i and Mississippi

LIST OF TABLES, ILLUSTRATIONS & FIGURES

LIST OF TABLES, ILLUSTRATIONS & FIGURES
(Continued)

LIST OF APPENDICES

An Analysis of the Impact of Healthcare Insurance Availability on Health Outcomes in Hawaiʻi and Mississippi

James G. Lenhart, M.D.

Chapter 1 – INTRODUCTION & BACKGROUND

The availability of healthcare insurance in the United States varies widely from jurisdiction to jurisdiction. State policy, employment/unemployment, eligibility requirements, means testing, poverty, disability, age, and gender factor significantly, and differently, from state to state (KFF, 2009). For example, a federal program called Medicaid insures pregnant women during pregnancy and childbirth in most states, but coverage for women of reproductive age often terminates post-partum (KFF, 2009). According to Fahrenthold (2006), some states mandate employers to provide health insurance to employees, most do not. Many jurisdictions provide insurance for children through Medicaid, but the extent and duration of coverage varies from state to state. Medicare, a federally sponsored health insurance program for senior citizens (those aged > 64 years), provides health insurance benefits for the "elderly", however, forty-seven million working Americans ages 18 to 65 went without health insurance in 2007 (Cantor, 2007).

This investigation compared, contrasted and analyzed the impact of healthcare insurance status on health outcomes in Hawaiʻi and Mississippi. If significant differences in outcomes are identified, healthcare policy changes to improve the availability of healthcare insurance state by state and nationwide will be recommended.

1.1 Healthcare Insurance in the United States

Healthcare insurance in the United States may categorically be divided into four major types (U.S. Census Bureau, 2009):

1. Employer based health insurance aka "commercial insurance" (insurance products brokered to employers and provided to employees as a benefit)

2. Public Employee Benefit Programs (PEBP) or government employee health insurance

3. State mandated, employer based health insurance

4. Public (government funded) insurance like Medicaid

1.2 Employer Based Health Insurance: Commercial Products and the Marketplace

In the U.S. employer based health insurance is a multi-billion dollar industry (CNN Money, 2009). Employers purchase employee benefit contracts from insurance companies who in turn market an array of products tailored to satisfy the budgetary limitations of companies large and small as well as employer appetite for providing comprehensive or more restrictive benefits. The potpourri of marketed insurance products can be mind boggling. For example, two of the largest health insurers in the state of Nevada each offer menus of over 19 products to satisfy marketplace demand for covered services, premiums, deductibles and co-pays as well as additions or subtractions for vision and dental benefits (HPN, 2009). None-the-less employer based commercial health insurance is tightly regulated.

1.21 Employer Based Health Insurance: Federal Regulation & Policy

Employees may receive health insurance as a benefit of employment depending on a variety of factors like job status, hours worked per pay period, union representation and employer policies. The U.S. Department of Labor Employee Benefits Security Administration (EBSA) provides regulatory oversight, which ensures fraud and abuse protections under the laws first enacted as Title I of the Employee Retirement Income Security Act of 1974 (EBSA, 2009).

According to its mission statement EBSA (2009) develops policies that "encourage" the expansion of employee healthcare benefits, correct violations of employee-employer statutes, provide employees access to information regarding benefit rights and assist employers in meeting their fiduciary responsibilities to the health of insured employees. Some examples of policies under the aegis of EBSA include:

- **The Health Insurance Portability and Accountability Act (HIPAA) of 1996** limits the ability of a new employer plan to exclude coverage for preexisting conditions; prohibits discrimination against employees based on prior medical conditions, previous claims experience, and genetic information; and guarantees that individuals will have access to, and can renew, individual health insurance policies (EBSA, 2009).

- **The Newborns' and Mother's Health Protection Act of 1996** states that health insurers "may not restrict benefits for a hospital stay in connection with childbirth to less than 48 hours following a vaginal delivery or 96 hours following a delivery by cesarean section" (EBSA, 2009).

- **The Women's Health and Cancer Rights Act (WHCRA) of 1998** under WHCRA health insurers offering mastectomy coverage for breast cancer must also provide coverage for reconstructive surgery (EBSA, 2009).

- **The Mental Health Parity Act (MHPA) of 1996** under the MHPA health insurers may not set "annual or lifetime dollar limits on mental health benefits that are lower than any such dollar limits for medical and surgical benefits" (EBSA, 2009).

In accordance with EBSA regulations, states may modify federal rules if state law is more protective than federal law.

1.22 Employer Based Health Insurance: State Regulation

States provide insurance regulation and oversight through state Insurance Commissions, which function through the National Association of Insurance Commissioners (NAIC, 2009). State Insurance Commissions enforce insurer compliance with State and Federal Laws. Insurance Commissions are charged with consumer protection – oversight for insurer financial reserves, insurer ability to meet obligations in worse case scenarios, insurer capacity to deliver on insurance policy provisions, and promotion of consumer protection legislation.

1.23 Employer Based Health Insurance: Hawai'i Regulation

The Hawai'i Department of Commerce and Consumer Affairs (HDCCA): Insurance Division in the state of Hawai'i is charged with protecting citizens from insurance fraud and malfeasance. "The division ensures that consumers are provided with insurance services meeting acceptable standards of quality, equity and dependability at fair rates by establishing and enforcing appropriate service standards" (HDCCA, 2009). The HDCCA Health Insurance Branch provides administrative support to the Patients' Rights and Responsibilities Act, which by law guarantees health insurance protections to the citizens of the State (HDCCA, 2009).

1.24 Employer Based Health Insurance: Mississippi Regulation

According to the Mississippi Insurance Department (MID) its mission is to "impartially enforce the laws and regulations enumerated in Mississippi Code Ann" (MID, 2009), which provides the citizens of Mississippi maximum consumer protection while creating a competitive marketplace for insurance products. The Department scrutinizes insurance companies licensed to conduct the business of insurance within the State with the aim of creating "the highest degree of economic security, quality of life, public safety and fire protection for the State's citizens at the lowest possible cost" (MID, 2009).

In summary, employer based health insurance regulation at the federal and state level serves for consumer protection, not consumer advocacy. In other words, commercial health insurance regulation at its many levels does not ensure health insurance availability for all employed individuals nor does it provide for depth and breadth of plans, which cover essential healthcare services.

1.3 Public Employee Benefits Programs (PEBP) Health Insurance

Employees of federal, state and local governmental agencies enjoy health insurance and retirement benefits. Provided under the auspices of Public Employee Benefits Programs, benefits are administered and regulated by the governmental entity that provides them. In other words, eligibility criteria as well as breadth and depth of coverage are based on policies established by the granting agency. Federal criteria and benefits may vary from state criteria and benefits, which may vary from county and city criteria within the same state. Eligibility and benefits criteria vary from state to state as well. The following bullet points compare and contrast the Public Employee Benefits Programs of Hawai'i and Mississippi illustrating the significant differences between each state.

1.31 Hawai'i Health Insurance Benefits under the Basic PEBP Plan (Hawaii Employer-Union Health Benefits Trust Fund, 2009)

Premiums

- Employee contributes $64 for self, $194 for family
- Employer contributes $209 for employee, $648 for family
- Total premium $273 for employee, $843 for family

Summary of Benefits under Plan

- Preventive check-ups $25/visit (mammography covered benefit)

- No lifetime maximum benefit

- Out of pocket limit $2000/individual

- Co-pays $25 per occurrence for diagnostic lab and x-ray

- Well child care $25 co-pay; immunizations no charge or $10

1.32 Mississippi Health Insurance Benefits under the Basic PEBP Plan (Employee Benefits and Services-Mississippi State University, 2009)

Premiums

- Employee contributes $0 for self, $517 for family

- Employer contributes $343 for employee, $343 for family

- Total premium $343 for employee, $860 for family

Summary of Benefits under Plan

- $1000 annual wellness/preventive healthcare coverage

- $1,000,000 lifetime maximum benefit for each participant

- $1,100 individual and $2,200 family deductible includes prescriptions

- Co-pays: 20%

- Well child care 100%, immunizations 80%

Table 1 compares employee out-of-pocket premiums as a percentage of median income and 300% of the Federal Poverty Level (FPL 300) and illustrates the impact of public policy health insurance status. For government employees insured under the state Public Employee Benefits Program in Hawai'i, the employee out-of-pocket premium for a basic family plan is 3.6% of median income and 2.2% of the FPL 300; in Mississippi the state Public Employee Benefits Program basic family plan out-of-pocket premium is 16.6% of median income and 10.4% of the FPL 300. The comprehensive plan for families in Hawai'i costs employees 5.7% of median income and 3.5% of the FPL 300, whereas the comprehensive plan for families in Mississippi out-of-pocket premium is 18.1% of median income and 11.4% of FPL 300. Despite Hawai'i's high median income and cost of living, health insurance premiums are not proportionately higher than other states including Mississippi.

Table 1: Public Employee Health Insurance Premium Rates Hawai'i & Mississippi Compared

	Basic Plan Monthly Premium						Comprehensive Plan Monthly Premium					
State	**Hawai'i**			**Mississippi**			**Hawai'i**			**Mississippi**		
Contributor	-ee	-er	tot	-ee	-er	tot	-ee	-er	tot	-ee	-er	tot
Self	$63	$209	$273	$0	$343	$343	$98	$209	$308	$0	$361	$361
Two-Party	$153	$508	$661	$339	$343	$682	$238	$508	$746	$385	$361	$746
Family	$194	$648	$843	$517	$343	$860	$304	$648	$952	$563	$361	$924
% Median Income	%		%	%		%	%		%	%		%
Self	1.2		5.1	0		11	1.8		5.8	0		11.6
Two-Party	2.9		12.4	10.9		21.9	4.4		13.9	12.3		23.9
Family	3.6		15.8	16.6		27.6	5.7		17.8	18.1		29.6
% of FPL												
Self	0.7		3.1	0		6.9	1.1		3.6	0		7.3
Two-Party	1.8		7.6	6.8		13.8	2.7		8.6	7.8		15.1
Family	2.2		9.7	10.4		17.4	3.5		10.9	11.4		18.7

Premium and benefits data adapted from:
Hawaii Employer-Union Health Benefits Trust Fund: Employer/Employee Contributions.
http://www.eutf.hawaii.gov/OE_2009/Interim_Rates_eff_7-1-09_to_12-31-09_County_Employees.pdf
and
Guide to Key Policies and Procedures, Employee Benefits and Services-Mississippi State University.
http://www.hrm.msstate.edu/benefits/benefitsoverview.html

Legend:
-ee = employee contribution
-er = employer contribution
tot = total monthly insurance premium (employee + employer)
% of Median Income = total annual premium as percent of state's annual median income
% of FPL = total annual premium as percent of income adjusted to 300% Federal Poverty Level

To summarize, basic and comprehensive PEBP health insurance plans are proportionately more affordable in Hawai'i than in Mississippi making health insurance coverage for PEBP employees in Hawai'i more accessible than PEBP employees in Mississippi.

1.4 State Mandated, Employer Based Health Insurance

In 1974 Hawai'i instituted the Prepaid Health Care Act (PHC) mandating employers to provide health insurance to full time employees (Mondragon, 1995). According to Buchmueller (2009), "the Hawai'i PHC Act was the first in the nation to set minimum standards of health care benefits for workers." The Prepaid Health Care Act (Appendix 4, p.77) specifically states "Employers must provide health care coverage to employees who work at least twenty (20) hours per week and earn 86.67 times the current Hawai'i minimum wage a month ($7.25 x 86.67 = $628). Coverage commences after four (4) consecutive weeks of employment or the earliest time thereafter at which coverage can be provided by the health care plan contractor, which is usually the first of the month" (Hawai'i Department of Labor and Industrial Relations [HDLIR], 2007). Employees may waive mandated coverage; if for example, they are covered by federally established health insurance like Medicare or Medicaid or a dependent under a qualified plan (HDLIR, 2007).

Like most U.S. states, Mississippi does not mandate employer based health insurance, making health insurance less available to residents of Mississippi than Hawaii as illustrated in Table 2.

1.41 The Impact of State Mandated Health Insurance on Insurance Prevalence

Table 2 compares and contrasts the impact of state mandated, employer based health insurance on health insurance prevalence. Nationwide the uninsured rate stands at 20.4%; in Mississippi, a state without an employer health insurance mandate, the uninsured rate is 24.1%. In Hawai'i and Massachusetts (two states with state mandated, employer health insurance) the uninsured rates are 10.7% and 7.3% respectively with over 70% of each state's population covered by employer based health insurance. Mississippi's employer based rate is just 55%.

Table 2: Health Insurance Prevalence in Adults Aged 19-64 years in the U.S. & Selected States

	Employer	Individual	Medicaid	Other Public	Uninsured	Total
United States	62%	5.8%	8.6%	3.2%	20.4%	100%
Hawai'i*	74.7%	3.2%	7.3%	4.1%	10.7%	100%
Mississippi	54.7%	5.3%	11.8%	4.1%	24.1%	100%
Massachusetts*	70.8%	4.5%	15.7%	1.6%	7.3%	100%

*States with employer mandated health insurance
Source: Adapted from The Henry J. Kaiser Family Foundation, 2009. State Health Facts

1.5 Public (government funded) health insurance: Medicaid

Medicaid, a federal program that provides health insurance through public funding, came into existence in 1965 under Title XIX of the Social Security Act. Medicaid provides healthcare benefits to certain vulnerable (and eligible) populations aged less than 65 years. The Kaiser Family Foundation (KFF), 2009 considers Medicaid "a linchpin in our health care system, covering health and long-term care services for millions of Americans, including many of the sickest and poorest. In 2005, Medicaid covered 59 million people, including one-quarter of U.S. children."

Over the past four decades, Medicaid has worked to alleviate healthcare access issues for the nation's poor, particularly children. Berk (1998) asserts "Medicaid is critical in mitigating many of the deprivations in access of poor persons who are eligible for public insurance. Once insurance status is controlled for, the poor are no more likely than the non-poor to be unable to obtain healthcare services."

The federal government and recipient states jointly finance Medicaid. The "Fed" matches state spending and, according to KFF (2009), there is no funding cap, "which allows federal funds to flow to states based on actual need. Through the matching system, the federal government and the states share the cost of the program" (KFF, 2009).

However, to receive federal matching funds, state Medicaid programs must cover certain "mandatory services" specified by federal law. Benefits include physician services, hospital and

9

laboratory services, preventive health services for individuals under 21, dental care, prescription medications, home health services and transportation services (KFF, 2009). Furthermore, Federal law requires states to cover certain "mandatory groups" in order to receive matching federal funds. Mandatory groups include pregnant women, children under age 6 with family income below 133% Federal Poverty Level, and children age 6 to 18 below 100% FPL. "Adults without dependent children, no matter how poor they are, are categorically excluded from Medicaid under federal law unless they are disabled or pregnant" (KFF, 2009). In other words, Medicaid eligibility hinges on means testing, which according to Baldock (2007) engenders feelings of shame, lack of self-respect and low esteem.

Administration of Medicaid programs defaults to recipient states with oversight by the Centers for Medicare and Medicaid Services (CMS) in the U.S. Department of Health and Human Services (KKF, 2009). While federal law outlines the "minimum requirements that all state Medicaid programs must fulfill… states have broad authority to define eligibility, benefits, provider payment, and other aspects of their programs." For example, states may enact certain federally qualified "optional" programs, which act to expand the depth and breadth of Medicaid services or they may fund programs at percentages higher than the minimum 133% FPL set by the "Feds". As a consequence, "Medicaid operates as more than 50 distinct programs" (KFF, 2009). This deference to "States rights" makes systemization of federally funded public healthcare programs difficult, if not impossible.

1.51 Medicaid: Hawai'i and Mississippi Compared

Table 3 compares and contrasts the impact of 2006 State Medicaid policies on availability of health care insurance in Hawai'i and Mississippi. According to the Kaiser Family Foundation (2009) adults represent 34.2% of Medicaid enrollees in Hawai'i and just 17.2% in

10

Mississippi. Working parents are eligible for Medicaid at 100% of the FPL in Hawai'i versus 46% of the Federal Poverty Level in Mississippi. Infants, children aged 1 to 5 and children aged 6 to 19 are covered at 300% of the FPL in Hawai'i; in Mississippi eligibility for infants, children aged 1 to 5 and children aged 6 to 19 is 185%, 133% and 100% of the Federal Poverty Level respectively. In other words, less restrictive policy makes health insurance coverage through Medicaid more available to adults and working families in Hawai'i, while children and parents of children in Mississippi must live at or near dire poverty to qualify for Medicaid healthcare benefits (see also Appendix 5, p.79).

Table 3: A Comparison of Medicaid in Hawai'i and Mississippi

Medicaid Enrollment	HI	MS	HI	MS	
Total Enrollment, FY2006	217,300	787,700	16.9	26.8	% of total residents
Children	95,000	398,700	43.7	50.6	% of Medicaid enrollees
Adults	74,300	135,400	34.2	17.2	% of Medicaid enrollees
Elderly	23,000	94,800	10.6	12.0	% of Medicaid enrollees
Disabled	25,000	158,800	11.5	20.2	% of Medicaid enrollees
% Enrolled in Managed Care, 2007	—	—	79.9	0.0	% of Medicaid enrollees
Medicaid Eligibility Levels by Annual Income and FPL, 2009	HI*	MS**	HI	MS	
Working Parents	$20,244	$8,064	100	46	% of FPL
Pregnant Women	$37,444	$32,560	185	185	% of FPL
Infants	$60,720	$32,560	300	185	% of FPL
Children 1-5	$60,720	$23,408	300	133	% of FPL
Children 6-19	$60,720	$17,600	300	100	% of FPL

*2009 Median Income Hawai'i = $64,193
**2009 Median Income Mississippi = $37,416
Adapted from: The Henry J. Kaiser Family Foundation, 2009. *Medicaid State Health Facts* Available at:
http://www.kaisernetwork.org/gsaresults/search?site=KFForgnopdfs&filter=0&output=xml_no_dtd&client=kff&sp
=kff&getfields=*&q=state%20health%20facts&no_pdf=1

1.6 Cost of Health Insurance and Healthcare in the United States

The cost of health insurance in the U.S. has risen substantially in the past decade leading to dramatic increases in uninsured adults under the age of 65 years. Many employers have increased the amount employees must contribute; some have eliminated healthcare insurance as

11

an employee benefit. These actions have combined to make health insurance unaffordable for many, resulting in increased prevalence of uninsured in the U.S. according to Cantor (2007). Based on annual census data in the period from 1999 through 2004, "the number of states where 23% or more of the adult population was uninsured *tripled* from 4 to 12… in all but 12 states, the uninsured rate for adults under 65 increased" (Cantor, 2007). In 2005 the uninsured rate of adults in the U.S. was 20.5% with lows in Minnesota (11%), Iowa (12.2%) and Hawai'i (12.8%) and highs in Oklahoma (25.5%), New Mexico (26.1%) and Texas (30.4%).

The cost of health insured as a percentage of median income varies remarkably from state to state and impacts the rate of uninsured as reflected in Table 4. The three states with the lowest

Table 4: Income & Rate of Uninsured and Insurance Costs in six U.S. states

Median Household Income (MHHI)			Percent of Adults Under age 65 Uninsured		Employer-based Insurance Premiums as Percent of MHHI		Health Insurance Premiums per Enrolled Employee
2004-2005			2004-2005		2003		2007
United States	$46,071		20.5%		14.9%		$3,705
State	**Income**	**Rank**	**Percent**	**Rank**	**Percent**	**Rank**	**Premium**
Minnesota	$56,098	7	11.0%	1	12.9%	7	$3,809
Iowa	$45,671	24	12.2%	2	13.1%	9	$3,561
Hawai'i	$58,854	3	12.8%	3	12.0%	2	$3,119
Oklahoma	$39,292	44	25.5%	48	17.1%	43	$3.644
New Mexico	$39,916	42	26.1%	49	19.7%	50	$3,401
Texas	$42,102	38	30.4%	50	18.4%	49	$3,781

Adapted from: Cantor, J., 2007. Aiming higher: results from a state scorecard on health system performance. *The Commonwealth Fund*

rate of uninsured adults are compared against the three states with the highest rate of uninsured adults. Insurance premiums are remarkably constant despite substantially lower median incomes in low income states, adding to the burden and overall impact of healthcare costs in less economically affluent regions.

In conclusion, health insurance in the U.S. is regulated to protect consumers from fraud and abuse. Regulation does not ensure coverage for essential health services. Employer based health insurance is brokered to employers through health insurance companies in a commercial and highly competitive marketplace. Public employee benefits programs (PEBP) are provided and overseen by the granting governmental agency without federal regulation at the state or local levels and vary remarkably jurisdiction to jurisdiction with respect to employee costs and coverage for essential services. Employer based and Medicaid plans vary state to state as well. Few states have state mandated employer health insurance. Although the federal government requires states participating in Medicaid to cover certain mandatory groups and services to qualify for federal funds, the Fed grants states substantial latitude in providing benefits under Medicaid programs. Defining health insurance status in the U.S. is no easy matter.

On a national level these characteristics contribute to a system of healthcare which is fragmented, if not broken. The consequence is wide variation in health insurance prevalence at national, state and local levels as well as substantial differences in depth and breadth of plans to ensure coverage for essential services. Such a system leads to wide variation in health outcomes from state to state and in aggregate contributes to unfavorable U.S. health outcomes compared to other countries internationally. The public health impact of health insurance prevalence in the U.S. is enormous.

Chapter 2 – LITERATURE REVIEW

2.1   Literature Search Strategy

The search strategy for this treatise was constructed in PubMed utilizing Keywords,

Boolean operators, MeSH terms, Synonyms and Limits as summarized in Figure 1. Relevant

articles were extensively retrieved through the University of Liverpool Online Library.

Figure 1: MPH Dissertation Search Strategy in PubMed

Keyword	PubMed Search Term	# of Citations
Health Insurance	"Insurance, Health"[Mesh Major Topic]	70455
Health outcomes	"Insurance, Health"[Mesh] AND "Outcome Assessment (Health Care)" [Mesh]	3204
Synonyms/Narrower Term	**PubMed Search Term**	**# of Citations**
Hawai'i	"Insurance, Health"[Mesh] AND "Outcome and Process Assessment (Health Care)"[Mesh]) AND "Hawaii" [Mesh]	4 (none were relevant)
Mississippi	"Insurance, Health"[Mesh] AND "Outcome Assessment (Health Care)"[Mesh]) AND "Mississippi"[Mesh]	3 (none were relevant
Alternate Strategy	**PubMed Search Term**	**# of Citations**
Health Insurance, Health Outcomes plus PubMed subheading Statistics and numerical data	"Insurance, Health"[Majr] AND "Outcome Assessment (Health Care)"[Majr] with PubMed Subheading: Statistics and numerical data	450 (several relevant)
Limits	**PubMed Search Term**	**# of Citations**
Meta-analysis, English, Young Adult: 19-24 years, Adult: 19-44 years, Middle Aged: 45-64 years, Middle Aged + Aged: 45+ years, published in the last 10 years	"Insurance, Health"[Majr] AND "Outcome Assessment (Health Care)"[Majr] with PubMed Subheading: Statistics and numerical data	0
Legislation, English, Young Adult: 19-24 years, Adult: 19-44 years, Middle Aged: 45-64 years, Middle Aged + Aged: 45+ years, published in the last 10 years	"Insurance, Health"[Majr] AND "Outcome Assessment (Health Care)"[Majr] with PubMed Subheading: Statistics and numerical data	0
Systematic Review, English, Young Adult: 19-24 years, Adult: 19-44 years, Middle Aged: 45-64 years, Middle Aged + Aged: 45+ years, published in the last 10 yrs	"Insurance, Health"[Majr] AND "Outcome Assessment (Health Care)"[Majr] with PubMed Subheading: Statistics and numerical data	2 (relevant citations)
Exploding & Expanding		
Exploded and expanded relevant citations through evaluation and retrieval of journal articles identified in search strategy as well as analysis of bibliographical citations in *America's health rankings, 2008* (United Health Foundation) and *Aiming higher: results from a state scorecard system, 2007* (The Commonwealth Fund) and others (see References).		

2.2 Healthcare Insurance & Access to Care in the United States

Cantor (2007) asserted that high performance healthcare is inextricably tied to access, making access the bedrock of healthcare in the U.S. Furthermore, he argued "The foremost factor in determining whether people have access to care when needed is having insurance that covers essential care." Several studies have demonstrated that quality of care is tied to access by improving measures on immunization rates for adults and children, cancer screening programs for colon and breast malignancies, and the care of chronic conditions like congestive heart failure and diabetes. Freeman (2008) for example demonstrated through systematic review that health insurance consistently increased healthcare utilization and improved health.

The incidence of premature death provides a trenchant example of the impact of access on outcomes. Premature death is defined as the loss of productive life due to death before age 75 – years of potential life lost (YPLL-75). According to the United Health Foundation (UHF) (2008), the age-adjusted national data for YPLL-75 is 6,000 years loss per 100,000 in states like Massachusetts, Minnesota, Hawai'i and Vermont, which rank high in the dimension of access and 10,000 years lost per 100,000 in states like Mississippi, Louisiana, and Alabama, which rank low in the dimension of access.

Getting the right care and receiving it at the right time may define access in sweeping terms; however, for scholarly analysis such a definition is too broad. The Commonwealth Fund (CF) defines access in terms of dimensions like the percentage of adults under age 65 who are insured, the percentage of children insured, the number of adults who visited a doctor in the past 2 years, and the number of adults without a time when they needed to see a doctor but could not because of cost. Bindman (1995) studied preventable hospitalizations and access to care; 6674 adults aged 18 through 64 were surveyed by ZIP code clusters for access to care, chronic healthcare conditions and their propensity to seek care. Bindman discovered that access to care was inversely associated with the hospital admission rates for chronic medical conditions like asthma, congestive heart failure, and diabetes ($p < 0.001$).

Substantial variation in health insurance plans from state to state characterizes U.S. healthcare coverage. Variations in Medicaid healthcare policies reflect this reality. In the U.S., Medicaid has operated as a federally funded public health insurance program since 1965. Under federal requirements states must meet certain mandatory coverage thresholds to qualify for Medicaid funds; however, states can opt to improve coverage beyond the mandatory floor. For example, mandatory coverage thresholds to qualify for funding in most instances are 133% of the Federal Poverty Level (FPL). Some states, like Massachusetts, cover children at family incomes at 300% of the FPL. In both the Commonwealth Fund and United Health Foundation studies Massachusetts ranked high in dimensions of access. In fact, Cantor (2007) asserts "The best performing states in the access dimension of performance are among those with the most expansive eligibility policies for public health insurance coverage."

Studies document that health insurance prevalence acts as a provocative health determinant. In regions where insurance prevalence is high, residents are more likely to receive preventive services and possess a medical home according to the Commonwealth Fund. Berk, et al (1998) analyzed the results of the 1994 Robert Wood Johnson Foundation National Access to Care Survey to determine the impact of Medicaid on health outcomes. The authors determined those unable to obtain one or more essential healthcare service over a one year period were uninsured 34%, Medicaid recipients 22% and privately insured 13%. The authors found similar rates regarding ability or inability to receive dental care, eyeglasses and prescription services.

Berk concluded the findings "indicate the potency of health insurance coverage as a policy lever in reducing financial barriers to care."

Not having health insurance has dire consequences. Andrulis (1998) argued that access to is "the centerpiece in the elimination of socioeconomic disparities in health" contending that lack of health insurance adversely affects health outcomes and quality of care. Hadley (1991) utilized multiple regression analysis to test for significant differences between 592,598 uninsured and privately insured patients (age-sex-race-specific-cohorts) admitted to U.S. hospitals in 1987. "The uninsured had a 44% to 124% higher risk of in-hospital mortality at the time of admission than did privately insured" (Hadley, 1991).

Inability to seek care and delay in care because of cost substantially increases the cost of care. Weissman (1991) analyzed data from 12,068 hospital admissions and concluded "The odds of delaying care because of costs for patients who were both poor and uninsured were 12 times greater than the odds for other patients ($p = .0001$). After controlling for diagnosis related groups (DRGs) and severity, patients who reported delays had 9% longer hospital stays compared with others ($p < 0.001$)." In 2009, the cost of a single hospital bed day in Las Vegas, Nevada was $1883 excluding physician charges for procedures.

2.3 Measuring Healthcare Outcomes in U.S. States: State Comparisons

According to the Commonwealth Fund (2007) the top five performing states in health outcomes were Hawaii, Iowa, New Hampshire, Vermont, and Maine; while the bottom five performing states were Nevada, Arkansas, Texas, Oklahoma, and Mississippi where:

1. The dimension of *access* was defined by rates of insurance for children and adults under 65 years;

2. *Quality* was defined by immunization and preventive services rates as well as appropriate care for congestive heart failure, pneumonia and myocardial infarction;

3. *Avoidable hospital use & costs* were defined by hospital readmission rates, frequency of hospital admissions for asthma and ambulatory conditions amenable to care;

4. *Equity* was defined by gaps in income and insurance status and;

5. The dimension of *healthy lives* was defined by mortality amenable to care, infant mortality, as well as cancer deaths for breast and colon cancer.

Although the United Health Foundation (UHF) utilized a different methodology to analyze U.S. state health outcomes, their findings supported Commonwealth Fund conclusions. Published as *America's Health Rankings, 2008,* the UHF ranked Vermont, Hawaii, New Hampshire, Minnesota, and Utah as the top 5 states while Texas, Tennessee, South Carolina, Mississippi, and Louisiana ranked 46th through 50th. The UHF analyzed health determinants to rank state by state health outcomes. Health determinants analyzed in the UHF study included:

1. Personal behaviors like smoking, drinking, and obesity;

2. Community factors like high school graduation rates, prevalence of violent crime, prevalence of infectious diseases, and the depth of poverty;

3. Public health & health policy factors like public health funding, the percentage of individuals without health insurance, and immunization rates and;

4. Clinical care determinants like the adequacy of prenatal care and the number of primary care physicians per 100,000 population.

Health outcomes analyzed in the UHF study included health dimensions like premature death; infant mortality; cardiovascular deaths; cancer deaths; geographic disparity and poor mental and physical health days.

UHF's *America's Health Rankings 2008* detailed the emergence of three themes. 1) access varies widely from state to state, 2) disparities in access to quality healthcare are increasing, and 3) uninsurance is a major roadblock to reducing health disparities (UHF, 2008).

2.4 Health Determinants: Hawai'i & Mississippi

The status of health determinants in Hawai'i and Mississippi is contrasted and compared in Table 5. Adapted from United Health Foundation, *America's Health Rankings, 2008* the table suggests substantial public policy differences in the two regions (see also Appendix 6, p.80).

Table 5: Health Determinants Hawai'i and Mississippi	HI	2008	MS	2008
HEALTH DETERMINANTS	**Value**	**Rank**	**Value**	**Rank**
Personal Behaviors				
Prevalence of Smoking (Percent of Population)	17.0	8	23.9	44
Prevalence of Binge Drinking (Percent of Population)	18.1	44	10.3	4
Prevalence of Obesity (Percent of Population)	21.7	2	32.6	50
Community & Environment				
High School Graduation (Percent of incoming 9th graders)	75.1	31	63.3	47
Violent Crime (Offense per 100,000 population)	273	12	291	18
Occupational Fatalities (Deaths per 100,000 workers)	5.5	22	11.1	46
Infectious Disease (Cases per 100,000 population)	15.6	30	18.2	35
Children in Poverty (Percent of persons under age 18)	11.6	5	32.8	50
Air Pollution (Micrograms of fine particles per cubic meter)	4.9	2	13.2	29
Public & Health Policies				
Lack of Health Insurance (Percent without health insurance)	8.2	2	19.8	46
Public Health Funding (Dollars per person)	$198	1	$61	31
Immunization Coverage (Percent of children ages 19 to 35 months)	87.8	4	78.7	34
Clinical Care				
Adequacy of Prenatal Care (Percent of pregnant women)	63.7	—	73.6	—
Primary Care Physicians (Number per 100,000 population)	146.9	7	81.5	48
Preventable Hospitalizations (Number per 1,000 Medicare enrollees)	32.2	1	109.8	47
ALL HEALTH DETERMINANTS	16.0	2	-10.5	49

Adapted from: United Health Foundation: America's Health Rankings, 2008. Available at: www.americashealthrankings.org/2008

Significant health determinant differences between the two states include public health funding, preventable hospitalizations, health insurance prevalence, immunization coverage, children in poverty, prevalence of obesity and number of primary care physicians per capita. Mississippi bests Hawai'i in only two of the sixteen categories – prevalence of binge drinking and adequacy of prenatal care. With respect to health determinants Hawai'i ranks 2nd nationally, Mississippi ranks 49th (UHF, 2008). The health determinant status of each state reflects back on UHF's health outcomes analysis state by state and nationally.

2.5 A Comparison of Health Outcomes in Hawai'i and Mississippi

Table 6 provides a comparison of sentinel health outcomes in the states of Hawai'i and Mississippi. This snap shot is based on UHF's analysis of health outcomes data. Rankings are benchmarked and compared against all fifty U.S. states, which equates to a national rank [see Appendices 7 & 8 (pp.82 & 83) for more detail on outcomes and state rankings].

Table 6: Comparison of Sentinel Health Outcomes for Hawai'i and Mississippi

	HAWAII	2008	MISSISSIPPI	2008
HEALTH OUTCOMES	**Value**	**Rank**	**Value**	**Rank**
Poor Mental Health Days (Days in previous 30 days)	2.8	7	4.0	49
Poor Physical Health Days (Days in previous 30 days)	2.9	4	4.0	44
Geographic Disparity (Relative standard deviation)	8.8	13	13	36
Infant Mortality (Deaths per 1,000 live births)	6.1	17	10.2	49
Cardiovascular Deaths (Deaths per 100,000 population)	241.1	2	387.0	50
Cancer Deaths (Deaths per 100,000 population)	159.0	1	215.2	46
Premature Death (Years lost per 100,000 population)	6,255	12	11,308	49
ALL HEALTH OUTCOMES	5.5	4	-4.5	50

Adapted from: United Health Foundation: America's Health Rankings, 2008. Available at: www.americashealthrankings.org/2008

2.6 Healthcare Outcomes in the United States: An International Comparison

Davis (2007) compared the health outcomes of Australia, Canada, Germany, the United Kingdom, New Zealand, and the United States. In her work, the U.S. performed last or next to last in measures like access, quality, healthy lives, patient safety, efficiency, and equity compared to the other five countries. "The U.S. health system is the most expensive in the world, but comparative analysis consistently show the United States underperforms relative to other countries on most dimensions of performance" (Davis, 2007). Davis concluded three features distinguish healthcare underperformance in the U.S. compared to the others: 1) lack of universal health insurance coverage, 2) limited adoption of health information technology and 3) marginal utilization of nurse case managers to coordinate the care of chronically ill.

Several other published works magnify the underperformance of U.S. healthcare compared to many developed countries. For example, Nolte (2003) determined that analyzed against European nations, the U.S. ranked 16th on overall mortality amenable to healthcare for disorders like colon and breast malignancies; diabetes; and ischemic heart disease. Sweden, Norway, Australia, Canada and France ranked 1st through 5th respectively in Nolte's analysis; of the nineteen countries analyzed only Ireland, the UK and Portugal ranked lower than the U.S.

The World Health Organization, *World Health Statistics 2008* compared the U.S. to other nations on a variety of measures like healthy life expectancy, infant mortality, cancer deaths, cardiovascular deaths, and obesity. Healthy life expectancy (HALE) measures the number of years a newborn can expect to live a healthy and productive life. Japan's HALE is 75 years and ranks 1st. On the flipside, the United States' HALE is 69 years – the same as Portugal and Slovenia – ranking it 28th compared to countries like Italy, Norway, Sweden, Germany, Greece, Ireland, France, and New Zealand (WHO, 2008).

According to *World Health Statistics 2008* (WHO, 2008) the U.S. underperforms in infant mortality as well. The U.S. infant mortality rate (IMR) was 7 deaths per 1,000 live births in 2008. The IMR for Japan, Sweden, Finland, Singapore, Italy, Norway, Denmark, Portugal, and the Czech Republic is 3 deaths per 1,000 live births.

Lavizzo-Mourey (2008) asserts that system faults are responsible for poor U.S. healthcare performance. "Everything we spend on healthcare supports a 'sick care' system of medical care and biomedical research. Less than 5% is for public health and prevention."

The literature suggests the reasons for U.S. healthcare underperformance internationally are many. However, the whole is equal to the sum of the parts, and in the U.S. healthcare performance is a reflection of state health outcomes taken in aggregate. This treatise will show that improved health insurance prevalence positively impacts health outcomes, and assert as a correlate, that U.S. health performance is tied to state by state health insurance characteristics.

2.7 Quantitative Studies Supporting the Research Methodology

Several published studies establish the validity of the research methodology utilized in this dissertation. Sox (1998) and co-workers Department of Health Policy and Management, Harvard School of Public Health utilized chi-square analysis to examine univariate associations between variables like insurance status, regular site of care, perceived health, and education. Multivariate logistic regression further analyzed the association between insurance status and identification of a personal physician as well as the weight and statistical significance of the co-variates. Sox concluded that physician status was a stronger predictor of access to care than insurance status. "Patients without a regular physician were at greater risk for delay in seeking care (odds ratio [OR] = 1.6, 95% confidence interval [CI] = 1.2, 2.1)" (Sox, 1998). Sox and his co-workers further concluded that uninsured patients were "significantly more likely to delay seeking care" and to "report no physicians visits" in the past year (see Appendix 9, p.85).

Qureshi (2000) studied women ages 40 to 49 to demonstrate the impact of ethnicity and socioeconomic factors on the prevalence of screening mammography. She analyzed self-reported data on 18,245 women who participated in the Behavioral Risk Factor Surveillance System (BRFSS) from 1992 to 1993. Independent variables included ethnicity, income, education, marital status, health insurance, healthcare access, alcohol and tobacco use; dependent variables centered about health outcomes, e.g. rates of cholesterol, Pap smear and mammographic screening.

"Univariate associations between variables were assessed using SUDAAN (Version 7.5). Associations significance at the $P < 0.05$ level were included in the multivariate analysis. Multiple logistic regression models were created to examine the relationship between routine screening mammography and the independent variables" (Qureshi, 2000). Qureshi concluded that women with health insurance and healthcare access problems had less likelihood of obtaining screening mammography (see Appendix 9, p.85).

Litaker, (2003) conducted an analysis of the association between managed care activity and individual access to care. "The primary source for individual-level data in the analysis was the 1998 Ohio Family Health Survey (OFHS)." Like the BRFSS, the OFHS is a telephone survey.

Litaker analyzed OFHS telephone survey data on 16,261 adults, aged 18 to 98 years. Study variables included healthcare access, level of managed care, insurance status, income, and health system factors like availability of regional care. In Litaker's analysis, "The X^2 test for homogeneity evaluated differences across levels of insurance for each factor and the X^2 test for trend assessed a dose-response relationship between managed care activity and unmet need controlling for insurance status." To refine the analysis, Litaker utilized multivariate, hierarchical logistic regression to assess the independent effect of managed care penetration on patterns of obtaining needed care. At publication Litaker (2003) asserted "Greater managed care activity is associated with unfavorable patterns of healthcare access despite an individual's insurance status" (see Appendix 9, p.85).

Shi (1994) examined the relationship between the availability of primary care and mortality rates and life expectancy. Shi analyzed secondary data sets from the National Center for Health Statistics utilizing SPSS and multivariate regression analysis. Total mortality rates, neonatal mortality, heart disease, cancer and life expectancy constituted dependent variables analyzed against environment, lifestyles, heredity and medical care. Shi concluded that "primary care is by far the most significant variable related to better health status."

Newacheck, (1998) conducted bivariate and multivariate analysis of the 1995 National Health Interview Survey (NHIS) data to analyze health access dynamics. The NHIS is a nationwide household survey conducted by the U.S. Bureau of the Census for the National Center of Health Statistics. Newacheck and his colleagues concluded "When compared to poor children without insurance, poor children with Medicaid experienced considerably better access and higher utilization rates."

Chapter 3 – METHODOLOGY

3.1 Research Question

What impact does healthcare insurance availability have on health outcomes in the states of Hawaiʻi and Mississippi?

3.2 Aims & Objectives

Study Aims
a) To determine the impact of healthcare insurance availability on healthcare outcomes in Hawaiʻi and Mississippi.

b) To recommend public policy that improves healthcare insurance prevalence.

c) To recommend public policy that improves health insurance plan characteristics.

Study Objectives
a) To compare, contrast and analyze the impact of healthcare insurance prevalence and health insurance plan characteristics on health outcomes in Hawaiʻi and Mississippi.

3.3 Research Outcomes

This research proposes to determine the impact of healthcare insurance prevalence on health outcomes in Hawaiʻi and Mississippi. It tests the hypothesis that health insurance status improves access to care and health outcomes.

3.4 Epistemology

This research takes a positivist perspective assuming that quantitative analysis of healthcare insurance prevalence in a defined region may be utilized to predict population health outcomes for that region. It is grounded in the belief that a quantitative analysis of healthcare insurance prevalence objectively edifies the impact of health insurance on health status among populations and is based on the belief that such analyses can be performed longitudinally on data that is recurrently collected and readily available. Moreover, it presumes that armed with this knowledge, government officials, healthcare administrators and health policy advocates could leverage similar methodologies to forge sustainable strategies that improve the health status of the people they serve and the localities for which they bear responsibility.

3.5 Ethics

This research did not involve the NHS or direct engagement with any human subjects. Information drawn from the Behavioral Risk Factor Surveillance System (BRFSS) is in the public domain and comprises the entire data analyzed in this study. This is a quantitative analysis of data extracted from the BRFSS; the ethics application and approval are documented in Appendices 2 & 3 respectively (pp.64 & 75).

3.6 Study Design

This was a quantitative analysis of 2007 Behavioral Risk Factor Surveillance System (BRFSS) "core" questionnaire data collected by the Health Department of Hawai'i and the Mississippi State Department of Health. BRFSS survey data was selected for this study based on its refined methodology, acknowledged validity, and acceptance among policy makers, healthcare academics and public health advocates as a tool to analyze and track health outcomes.

In this study, self-reported, weighted BRFSS data from the states of Hawai'i and Mississippi on persons aged 19 through 64 were downloaded and analyzed. Tests of independence were calculated for health insurance status (the independent variable) and the selected dependent and confounding variables. Subsequently, self-reported weighted health insurance data from both states was subjected to bivariate analysis against the following self-reported weighted health outcomes data (the specific dependent variables):

- Delay in care due to costs;

- Identification of a personal doctor or healthcare provider;

- Prevalence of asthma;

- Prevalence of diabetes;

- Length of time since last regular check-up;

- Immunization rates for influenza, pneumococcal pneumonia and hepatitis B and;

- Health status.

Data was analyzed with SPSS Predictive Analytic Software v. 17.0. The SPSS Complex Samples module was utilized to reduce bias and facilitate management of multi-stage stratified samples like those integral to the BRFSS. Cross tabulations were run for the variables of interest for Hawai'i and Mississippi and analyzed using Roa-Scott adjusted chi-square to account for differences in variance and to determine significant values.

Delay in care due to costs and rates of influenza vaccination were further assessed with multivariate analysis of covariates utilizing logistic regression models. The strategy for the multivariate analysis models was based on statistical significance as well as relevance – delay in care due to cost (access to care) and public health impact (influenza immunization rates). The co-variates health care insurance, marital status, gender, age, income, education, employment and race were subjected to the multivariate, logistic regression analysis. Results were calculated as odds ratios within 95% confidence interval.

3.7   Data Source – The Behavioral Risk Factor Surveillance System (BRFSS)

This study analyzed secondary data extracted from the results of the 2007 Behavioral Risk Factor Surveillance System (BRFSS) survey for the states of Hawai'i and Mississippi. BRFSS data is available on the public domain. For this study 2007 BRFSS data was downloaded directly into SPSS from its source, the Centers for Disease Control and Prevention (CDC).

In 1984, the CDC established the Behavioral Risk Factor Surveillance System (BRFSS) as a collaborative project between the CDC and U.S. states. The BRFSS is a state-specific telephone survey that collects data on preventive health practices, health risk behaviors, and health care access. "More than 350,000 adults are interviewed each year, making the BRFSS the largest telephone health survey in the world. States use BRFSS data to identify emerging health problems, establish and track health objectives, and develop and evaluate public health policies and programs" (CDC, 2009). In addition, several states use System data to promote health-related legislative efforts according to the CDC. As a testament to its effectiveness and impact, in just over a decade all 50 states had adopted and continue to utilize the BRFSS to develop annual health outcomes data.

According to the CDC BRFSS (2007), the BRFSS questionnaire is divided into three components: 1) the "core" questionnaire: a standard set of questions surveyed by all states, 2) the optional modules: sets of CDC supported questions regarding specific healthcare issues that states may elect to utilize in the survey process and 3) the state added questions: developed by individual states, but not supported, edited or analyzed by the CDC. States develop their questionnaires in cooperative agreement with the CDC, ensuring a methodology that permits comparative analysis state by state. "Each year, the states and the CDC agree on the content of the core component and optional modules... new questionnaires are implemented in January and usually remain unchanged throughout the year" (CDC BRFSS, 2007). The CDC requires states to ask the core content questions without modification (Appendix 10, p.86).

In addition to demographic data, typical questions on the core component BRFSS include: Do you have any kind of health care coverage? Was there a time in the past 12 months you needed to see a doctor, but could not because of the cost? Have you had a flu shot in the last

12 months? Have you been told by a doctor, nurse or other health professional that you had asthma? Have you ever been told by doctor that you have diabetes? Have you ever had a mammogram? Have you smoked at least 100 cigarettes in your entire life? Have you participated in any physical activities such as running, calisthenics, golf, gardening, or walking for exercise outside of regular job during the past 30 days? Surveys are conducted monthly throughout the year in all states. All data is electronically transmitted to the CDC where it is processed, weighted and analyzed.

Data are self-reported, however, the validity of the surveillance methodology is well established and considered representative of adults who have telephones. According to the CDC telephone ownership ranges from 87 to 98 per cent across states, with households in the South and minorities having lower coverage. "No direct method of compensating for non-telephone coverage is employed by the BRFSS, however, post-stratification weights are used, which may partially correct for any bias caused by non-telephone coverage" (CDC BRFSS, 2007).

Several methodological features augment the validity of the BRFSS: 1) disproportionate stratified sampling, which enhances the probability that the sample is representative of all households, 2) random digit dialing through Computer-Assisted Telephone Interview (CATI) Systems, 3) disproportionate sampling of strata to account for geographical regions with rural populations, 4) training and monitoring interviewer performance, 5) conducting interviews every month throughout the calendar year, seven days per week, daytime and evening, 6) processing data monthly as electronically submitted, 7) CDC tracking of data from states monthly, and 8) post-stratification weighting of data (Appendix 10, p.86).

3.71 Data Source – The Hawaiʻi Behavioral Risk Factor Surveillance System

The Hawaii Behavioral Risk Factor Surveillance System (HBRFSS) was integrated into the national Behavioral Risk Factor Surveillance System (BRFSS) early in the inception of the BRFSS. The Hawaiʻi BRFSS telephone survey follows the national BRFSS protocol. Since 1986 the survey has analyzed self-reported demographic, health access, health behavior and health outcomes data on the people of Hawaiʻi. Hawaiʻi utilizes CATI random digit dialing to facilitate interviews and in 2007 utilized disproportionate sampling of strata to account for geographical regions within its rural populations (CDC BRFSS, 2007).

3.72 Data Source – The Mississippi Behavioral Risk Factor Surveillance System

Like other states the Mississippi BRFSS is a random sample telephone survey of adults 18 and over. Mississippi uses the CATI system of random digit dialing to conduct the surveys. According to Mississippi State Department of Health (MSDH), the survey has the potential to reach 93% of all households in Mississippi that have telephones. The survey is conducted on an ongoing basis throughout the year. "A sample size of between approximately 4,000 and 5,000 persons is selected each year to give a 95% confidence interval of ±3% or less on risk factor prevalence estimates of the adult population" (MSDH, 2009). The Mississippi State Department of Health claims a survey response rate of greater than 90%. In 2007, Mississippi utilized disproportionate sampling of strata to account for geographical regions within its rural populations (CDC BRFSS, 2007).

Chapter 4 – RESULTS

4.1 Analysis of BRFSS Data

Analytic results of the independent and dependent variables compare Hawai'i and Mississippi in Tables 7 through 17. In Table 7, the Roa-Scott adjusted chi-square univariate analysis of the independent variable "Do you have any kind of health care coverage, including health insurance, pre-paid plans such as HMOs or government plans such as Medicare?" is illustrated. In the 2007 BRFSS survey 92.9% (95% CI 91.7% - 93.7%) of Hawai'ians studied had health insurance; whereas in Mississippi 77.1% (95% CI 75.3% - 78.7%) had health insurance. This was significant at $p < 0.001$. For comparative purposes these data contrast with the rate of health insurance in the U.S. nationwide, which is tabulated (84.4%).

Table 7: Univariate Analysis of the Independent Variable

Chi-square Univariate Analysis					
Independent Variable		Hawai'i	Mississippi	p-value	U.S.*
Do you have any kind of health care coverage, including health insurance, pre-paid plans such as HMOs or government plans such as Medicare?	Estimate	92.9%	77.1%	< 0.001	84.4%
	95% CI				
	Lower	91.7%	75.3%		
	Upper	93.9%	78.7%		

* From the Center for Disease Control and Prevention, 2007. Behavioral Risk Factor Surveillance System: 2007 Codebook Report. [Online] Available at: http://www.cdc.gov/brfss/technical_infodata/surveydata/2007.htm

In this treatise, several BRFSS 2007 survey questions were selected as dependent variables and subjected to Roa-Scott adjusted chi-square bivariate analysis against the independent variable "Do you have any kind of health care coverage, including health insurance, pre-paid plans such as HMOs or government plans such as Medicare?" The results of the analysis are compared in Tables 8 through 17.

The data in Table 8 illustrate the impact of health insurance on access to care. In both Hawai'i and Mississippi having health insurance mitigated the need to delay care due to cost, significant at p < 0.001; 5.2% in Hawai'i (95% CI 4.4% - 6.1%) v. 14.2% in Mississippi (95% CI 12.7% - 16.0%).

Table 8: Impact of Health Insurance on Delay in Care Due to Costs – χ^2 Bivariate Analysis

Was there a time in the last twelve months you needed to see a doctor but could not because of cost?				Had to Delay Care Due to Cost	p value
Hawai'i	Have Health Insurance Coverage	95% Confidence Interval	Estimate	5.2%	< 0.001
			Lower	4.4%	
			Upper	6.1%	
Mississippi	Have Health Insurance Coverage	95% Confidence Interval	Estimate	14.2%	< 0.001
			Lower	12.7%	
			Upper	16.0%	

Table 9 compares the impact of health insurance on identification of a personal health care provider. In both Hawai'i 71.2% (95% CI 69.3% - 73%) and Mississippi 65.9% (95% CI 63.8% - 73.0%) having health insurance improved identification of a personal doctor or healthcare provider, significant at p < 0.001.

Table 9: Impact of Health Insurance on Identification of a Personal Provider – χ^2 Bivariate Analysis

Do you have one person you think of as your personal doctor or healthcare provider?				Have one Health Care Provider	p value
Hawai'i	Have Health Insurance Coverage	95% Confidence Interval	Estimate	71.2%	< 0.001
			Lower	69.3%	
			Upper	73.0%	
Mississippi	Have Health Insurance Coverage	95% Confidence Interval	Estimate	65.9%	< 0.001
			Lower	63.8%	
			Upper	73.0%	

Table 10 compares the impact of health insurance on length of time since last medical check-up. In both Hawai'i and Mississippi having health insurance improved frequency of routine check- ups, significant at p < 0.001.

Table 10: Impact of Health Insurance on Length of Time since Last Check-up – x^2 Bivariate Analysis

About how long has it been since you last visited a doctor for a routine checkup (within the last year)?				Have Routine Check-up in the Last Year	p value
Hawai'i	Have Health Insurance Coverage	95% Confidence Interval	Estimate	67.2%	< 0.001
			Lower	65.2%	
			Upper	69.1%	
Mississippi	Have Health Insurance Coverage	95% Confidence Interval	Estimate	69.3%	< 0.001
			Lower	67.2%	
			Upper	71.2%	

The 2007 BRFSS data on Hawai'i and Mississippi in Table 11 contrasts the impact of health insurance on identification of diabetes, a chronic condition with the potential for serious co-morbidities and reduction in healthy life expectancy. Health insurance had significant impact on the identification of diabetes in Mississippi 9.0% (95% CI 8.1% - 10.0%); p=0.006. However, health insurance status was not a significant factor in the diagnosis of diabetes in Hawai'i 5.5% (95% CI 4.7% - 6.4%); p=0.944.

Table 11: Impact of Health Insurance on told you have Diabetes – x^2 Bivariate Analysis

Have you ever been told by your doctor you have diabetes?				Have been told by Doctor I Have Diabetes	p value
Hawai'i	Have Health Insurance Coverage	95% Confidence Interval	Estimate	5.5%	0.944
			Lower	4.7%	
			Upper	6.4%	
Mississippi	Have Health Insurance Coverage	95% Confidence Interval	Estimate	9.0%	0.006
			Lower	8.1%	
			Upper	10.0%	

The data on Hawai'i and Mississippi in Table 12 compare the impact of health insurance on identification of asthma, a chronic condition with the potential for serious complications and reduction in healthy life expectancy. Health insurance did not have a significant impact on the identification of asthma in either Hawai'i p=0.087 or Mississippi p=0.847; Hawai'i 14.5% (95% CI 13.1% - 16.0%) and Mississippi 10.8% (95% CI 9.6% - 12.2%).

Table 12: Impact of Health Insurance on told you have Asthma – x^2 Bivariate Analysis

Have you ever been told by your doctor you have asthma?				Have been told by Doctor I Have Asthma	p value
Hawai'i	Have Health Insurance Coverage		Estimate	14.5%	0.087
		95% Confidence Interval	Lower	13.1%	
			Upper	16.0%	
Mississippi	Have Health Insurance Coverage		Estimate	10.8%	0.847
		95% Confidence Interval	Lower	9.6%	
			Upper	12.2%	

Table 13 illustrates the impact of health insurance on a critical public health dimension, influenza immunization. In both Hawai'i and Mississippi health insurance status improved influenza immunization rates, significant at $p < 0.001$.

Table 13: Impact of Health Insurance on Influenza Immunization – x^2 Bivariate Analysis

A flu shot is an influenza vaccine injected into your arm. During the past 12 months, have you had a flu shot?				Have had Flu Shot in the past 12 Months	p value
Hawai'i	Have Health Insurance Coverage		Estimate	38.5%	< 0.001
		95% Confidence Interval	Lower	36.6%	
			Upper	40.5%	
Mississippi	Have Health Insurance Coverage		Estimate	34.2%	< 0.001
		95% Confidence Interval	Lower	32.2%	
			Upper	36.2%	

The data in Table 14 compare the impact of health insurance on a critical public health dimension, pneumococcal pneumonia immunization. Healthcare insurance status improved

Table 14: Impact of Health Insurance on Pneumococcal Immunization – x^2 Bivariate Analysis

A pneumonia shot or pneumococcal vaccine is usually given only once or twice in a person's lifetime and is different from a flu shot. Have you ever had a pneumonia shot?				Have had the Pneumococcal Vaccine	p value
Hawai'i	Have Health Insurance Coverage		Estimate	16.0%	0.750
		95% Confidence Interval	Lower	14.5%	
			Upper	17.6%	
Mississippi	Have Health Insurance Coverage		Estimate	18.7%	0.013
		95% Confidence Interval	Lower	17.2%	
			Upper	20.4%	

pneumococcal pneumonia immunizations rates in Mississippi but not Hawaiʻi. Mississippi had pneumococcal pneumonia immunization rates of 18.7% (95% CI 17.2% - 20.4%); p=0.013 v. pneumococcal immunization rates of 16.0% in Hawaiʻi (95% CI 14.5% - 17.6%); p=0.750.

The data in Table 15 illustrate the impact of health insurance on a critical public health dimension, hepatitis B immunization. Health insurance improved hepatitis B immunization rates in Mississippi but not Hawaiʻi. Mississippi had hepatitis B immunization rates of 35.3% (95% CI 33.1% - 37.5%); p=0.041. Although proportionately more Hawaiʻians received hepatitis B shots

Table 15: Impact of Health Insurance on Hepatitis – x^2 Bivariate Analysis

Have you ever received the hepatitis B vaccine? The hepatitis B vaccine is completed after the third shot is given?				Have had the Hepatitis B Vaccine	p value
Hawaiʻi	Have Health Insurance Coverage		Estimate	48.8%	0.064
		95% Confidence Interval	Lower	46.6%	
			Upper	50.9%	
Mississippi	Have Health Insurance Coverage		Estimate	35.3%	0.041
		95% Confidence Interval	Lower	33.1%	
			Upper	37.5%	

compared to residents of Mississippi, the impact of health insurance on hepatitis B immunization rates in Hawaiʻi was not significant. Hawaiʻi hepatitis B immunization rates were 48.8% (95% CI 46.6% - 50.9%); p=0.064.

Table 16 compares the impact of health insurance on perceived health status. It reflects the percentage of those surveyed who had health insurance and perceived their health as excellent. Residents with health insurance perceived their health to be excellent at nearly the same proportion in both states – 21.1% in Hawaiʻi (95% CI 19.5% - 22.8%); p=0.004 and 19.8% Mississippi (95% CI 18.1% - 21.5%); p < 0.001.

Table 16: Impact of Health Insurance on Health Status Excellent – x^2 Bivariate Analysis

Would you say that your General Health is Excellent?				General Health Excellent	p value
Hawai'i	Have Health Insurance Coverage	95% Confidence Interval	Estimate	21.1%	0.004
			Lower	19.5%	
			Upper	22.8%	
Mississippi	Have Health Insurance Coverage	95% Confidence Interval	Estimate	19.8%	< 0.001
			Lower	18.1%	
			Upper	21.5%	

The percentage of those who had health insurance yet perceived their health to be poor is portrayed in Table 17. 5.5% of surveyed Mississippians perceived their health to be poor, despite health insurance status. Health insurance was not found to be a mitigating factor in people who perceived their health as poor in Mississippi p=0.785. In Hawai'i 2.2% of surveyed Hawai'ians with health insurance perceived their health to be poor. This was significant at p=0.016. The data suggests that having health insurance in Hawai'i was effective in mitigating perceptions of poor health status in Hawai'i, where it was not in Mississippi.

Table 17: Impact of Health Insurance on Health Status Poor – x^2 Bivariate Analysis

Would you say that your General Health is Poor?				General Health Poor	p value
Hawai'i	Have Health Insurance Coverage	95% Confidence Interval	Estimate	2.2%	0.016
			Lower	1.7%	
			Upper	2.8%	
Mississippi	Have Health Insurance Coverage	95% Confidence Interval	Estimate	5.5%	0.785
			Lower	4.7%	
			Upper	6.4%	

Table 18 provides a tabulated summary of the tests of independence for the bivariate analysis.

Table 18: Bivariate Statistical Results – Tabulated Summary of Tests of Independence

Hawai'i					
Variable	Chi Sq	Adj. F	df1	df2	Sig
Could not see a doctor because of cost - Have any kind of health care coverage	462.994	216.279	1	5016	< 0.001
Have personal healthcare provider - Have any kind of health care coverage	527.138	113.783	1.990	9982.185	< 0.001
Length of time since last check-up - Have any kind of health care coverage	231.795	31.191	2.917	14630.31	< 0.001
Ever been told you have diabetes - Have any kind of health care coverage	0.653	0.127	2.998	15038.426	0.994
Ever been told you have asthma - Have any kind of health care coverage	9.889	2.931	1	5016.000	0.087
Had an Influenza Shot past 12 months - Have any kind of health care coverage	58.266	23.520	1	5016	< 0.001
Had a Pneumococcal Immunization - Have any kind of health care coverage	0.347	0.102	1	5016	0.750
Had the hepatitis B vaccine - Have any kind of health care coverage	8.707	3.422	1	5016	0.064
Overall health described as excellent - Have any kind of health care coverage	34.053	3.941	3.842	19273.122	0.004
Overall health described as poor - Have any kind of health care coverage	10,722	5.850	1	5016	0.016

Mississippi					
Variable	Chi Sq	Adj. F	df1	df2	Sig
Could not see a doctor because of cost - Have any kind of health care coverage	515.938	220.161	1	5413.000	< 0.001
Have personal healthcare provider - Have any kind of health care coverage	306.627	80.604	1.752	9482.070	< 0.001
Length of time since last check-up - Have any kind of health care coverage	262.659	39.066	2.987	16168.269	< 0.001
Ever been told you have diabetes - Have any kind of health care coverage	15.629	4.196	2.876	15566.501	0.006
Ever been told you have asthma - Have any kind of health care coverage	0.083	0.037	1	5413.000	0.847
Had an Influenza Shot past 12 months - Have any kind of health care coverage	124.212	48.697	1	5413	< 0.001
Had a Pneumococcal Immunization - Have any kind of health care coverage	14.564	6.230	1	5413	0.013
Had the hepatitis B vaccine - Have any kind of health care coverage	10.517	4.164	1	5413.000	0.041
Overall health described as excellent - Have any kind of health care coverage	58.391	7.001	3.811	20626.712	< 0.001
Overall health described as poor - Have any kind of health care coverage	0.115	0.075	1	5413	0.785

The adjusted F is a variant of the second order Roa-Scott adjusted Chi-Square statistic. Significance is based on the adjusted F and its degrees of freedom

4.2 Logistic Regression Analysis

Delay in care due to costs and rates of influenza vaccination were subjected to analysis of covariates utilizing multivariate logistic regression models. The rationale for the multivariate analysis models were based on statistical significance found in the bivariate analysis as well as relevance – access to care (delay in care due to costs) and health insurance impact on a public health dimension (influenza immunization).

4.21 Delay in Care Due to Costs - Logistic Regression Model

In the first logistic regression model, delay in care due to cost was analyzed against the co-variates health insurance status, marital status, gender, age, income, education and race. Results were calculated as odds ratios within 95% confidence interval. As Table 19 illustrates the logistic regression analysis supported the findings of the bivariate analysis, health insurance mitigates delay in care due to costs in both Hawai'i OR=8.093 (95% CI 5.237 - 12.507); p <0.001 and Mississippi OR=3.221 (95% CI 2.489 - 4.168); p < 0.001 despite co-factors.

Table 19: Impact of Health Insurance on Delay in Care due to Costs – Logistic Regression

Could not see a doctor because of cost.				Odds Ratio	P value
Hawai'i	Have Health Insurance Coverage	95% Confidence Interval	Estimate	8.093	< 0.001
			Lower	5.237	
			Upper	12.507	
Mississippi	Have Health Insurance Coverage	95% Confidence Interval	Estimate	3.221	< 0.001
			Lower	2.489	
			Upper	4.168	

Dependent Variable: DELAY IN CARE DUE TO COSTS (referent category = no)
Model: (Intercept) Health Plan=yes, Marital Status=married, Gender=male, Age=imputed, Income=$50,000 or more, Employed=working, Education=college graduate, Race=white, non-Hispanic

Moreover, the logistic regression analysis supports the hypothesis (Illustration 1) that the prevalence of health insurance in Hawai'i compared to Mississippi significantly improved access to care (delay in care due to cost) in Hawai'i compared to Mississippi; odds ratios Hawai'i 8.093 (95% CI 5.237 - 12.507); Mississippi 3.271 (95% CI 2.489 - 4.168); p=0.000036.

38

Illustration 1: Calculating the p value Supporting the Hypothesis

Wald Chi-square = $[(b_1 - b_2)^2] / \{[se(b_1)]^2 + [se(b_2)]^2\}$ where the betas (b) for delay in care due to costs were the calculated logit coefficients for each Hawai'i (b_1) and Mississippi (b_2) divided by the square of standard errors (se) corresponding to each state. The p value was derived from CHIDIST in Microsoft Excel (Wald Chi-square, 1).

Wald chi-square = $[(b_1 - b_2)]^2 / \{[se_{b1}]^2 + [se_{b2}]^2\}$

Wald chi-square = $[(-2.091) - (-1.770)]^2 / \{[0.222]^2 + [0.132)]^2\}$

Wald chi-square = 12.715731

p value calculated from Wald chi-square (1 degree of freedom) = 0.000036

Table 20 reveals that male gender was found to be a confounding factor in delay of care due to costs in Mississippi OR=1.619 (95% CI 1.216 - 2.076); $p < 0.001$ but not Hawai'i OR=1.266 (95% CI 0.911 - 1.760); $p = 0.161$.

Table 20: Impact of Gender on Delay in Care due to Costs – Logistic Regression

Could not see a doctor because of cost.				Odds Ratio	p value
Hawai'i	Gender = Male		Estimate	1.266	0.161
		95% Confidence Interval	Lower	0.911	
			Upper	1.760	
Mississippi	Gender = Male		Estimate	1.619	< 0.001
		95% Confidence Interval	Lower	1.263	
			Upper	2.076	

Dependent Variable: DELAY IN CARE DUE TO COSTS (referent category = no)
Model: (Intercept) Health Plan=yes, Marital Status=married, Gender=male, Age=imputed, Income=$50,000 or more, Employed=working, Education=college graduate, Race=white, non-Hispanic

Income was a confounding variable in both Hawai'i and Mississippi relative to delay in care due to costs. This is illustrated categorically by income levels in Table 21.

Table 21: Impact of Income on Delay in Care due to Costs – Logistic Regression

Could not see a doctor because of cost.				Odds Ratio	p value
Hawaiʻi	Income Missing vs. $50,000 or more	95% Confidence Interval	Estimate	1.276	0.554
			Lower	0.570	
			Upper	2.855	
Hawaiʻi	Less than $15,000 vs. $50,000 or more	95% Confidence Interval	Estimate	5.474	< 0.001
			Lower	3.013	
			Upper	9.943	
Hawaiʻi	$15,000 to less than $25,000 vs. $50,000 or more	95% Confidence Interval	Estimate	3.275	< 0.001
			Lower	1.971	
			Upper	5.444	
Hawaiʻi	$25,000 to less than $35,000 vs. $50,000 or more	95% Confidence Interval	Estimate	1.933	0.014
			Lower	1.144	
			Upper	3.264	
Hawaiʻi	$35,000 to less than $50,000 vs. $50,000 or more	95% Confidence Interval	Estimate	2.094	0.002
			Lower	1.309	
			Upper	3.349	
Could not see a doctor because of cost.				**Odds Ratio**	**p value**
Mississippi	Income Missing vs. $50,000 or more	95% Confidence Interval	Estimate	2.964	< 0.001
			Lower	1.807	
			Upper	4.862	
Mississippi	Less than $15,000 vs. $50,000 or more	95% Confidence Interval	Estimate	6.647	< 0.001
			Lower	4.474	
			Upper	9.875	
Mississippi	$15,000 to less than $25,000 vs. $50,000 or more	95% Confidence Interval	Estimate	5.105	< 0.001
			Lower	3.556	
			Upper	7.330	
Mississippi	$25,000 to less than $35,000 vs. $50,000 or more	95% Confidence Interval	Estimate	3.697	< 0.001
			Lower	2.488	
			Upper	5.494	
Mississippi	$35,000 to less than $50,000 vs. $50,000 or more	95% Confidence Interval	Estimate	2.658	< 0.001
			Lower	1.846	
			Upper	3.828	

Dependent Variable: DELAY IN CARE DUE TO COSTS (referent category = no)
Model: (Intercept) Health Plan=yes, Marital Status=married, Gender=male, Age=imputed, Income=$50,000 or more, Employed=working, Education=college graduate, Race=white, non-Hispanic

In the logistic regression model the impact of education on delay in care due to costs was found to be a significant confounding factor in Mississippi, but not Hawaiʻi. Table 22 illustrates that graduating from college in Mississippi OR=1.421 (95% CI 1.078 - 1.874); p=0.013 or some college 1.410 (95% CI 1.029 - 1.931); p=0.032 improved delay in care due to costs, but did not

Table 22: Impact of Education on Delay in Care due to Costs – Logistic Regression

Could not see a doctor because of cost.				Odds Ratio	p value
Hawai'i	High School or less vs. College Graduate or more	95% Confidence Interval	Estimate	1.404	0.100
			Lower	0.938	
			Upper	2.102	
Hawai'i	Some College vs. College Graduate or more	95% Confidence Interval	Estimate	1.196	0.397
			Lower	0.791	
			Upper	1.808	
Mississippi	High School or less vs. College Graduate or more	95% Confidence Interval	Estimate	1.421	0.013
			Lower	1.078	
			Upper	1.874	
Mississippi	Some College vs. College Graduate or more	95% Confidence Interval	Estimate	1.410	0.032
			Lower	1.029	
			Upper	1.931	

Dependent Variable: DELAY IN CARE DUE TO COSTS (referent category = no)
Model: (Intercept) Health Plan=yes, Marital Status=married, Gender=male, Age=imputed, Income=$50,000 or more, Employed=working, Education=college graduate, Race=white, non-Hispanic

impact delay in care due to costs in Hawai'i OR=1.404 (95% CI 0.938 - 2.102); p=0.100 and 1.196 (95% CI 0.791 - 1.808); p=0.392.

Age, marital status, employment and race were not found to be significant confounding factors in the multivariate logistic regression analysis for delay in care due to costs.

4.22 Influenza Immunization - Logistic Regression Model

In the second logistic regression model, influenza immunization status was analyzed against the co-variates health insurance status, marital status, gender, age, income, education and race. Results were calculated as odds ratios within 95% confidence intervals. As Table 23 illustrates, the logistic regression analysis supported the findings of the bivariate analysis, i.e. health insurance improved influenza immunization rates in both Hawai'i OR=0.376 (95% CI 0.236 – 0.598); p < 0.001 and Mississippi OR=0.516 (95% CI 0.389 – 0.683); p < 0.001 despite possible confounding factors like marital status, gender, age, education and race.

Table 23: Impact of Health Insurance on Influenza Immunization – Logistic Regression

Influenza Immunization in the Past 12 months.				Odds Ratio	p value
Hawaiʻi	Have Health Insurance Coverage	95% Confidence Interval	Estimate	0.376	< 0.001
			Lower	0.236	
			Upper	0.598	
Mississippi	Have Health Insurance Coverage	95% Confidence Interval	Estimate	0.516	< 0.001
			Lower	0.389	
			Upper	0.683	

Dependent Variable: INFLUENZA IMMUNIZATION (referent category = no)
Model: (Intercept) Health Plan=yes, Marital Status=married, Gender=male, Age=imputed, Income=$50,000 or more, Employed=working, Education=college graduate, Race=white, non-Hispanic

The data did not support the hypothesis that increased prevalence of health insurance in Hawaiʻi compared to Mississippi significantly improved immunization outcomes in Hawaiʻi compared to Mississippi. The p value was calculated from the Wald chi-square (Illustration 2).

Illustration 2: Calculating the p value for Influenza Immunization

$$\text{Wald chi-square} = [(b_1 - b_2)]^2 / \{[se_{b1}]^2 + [se_{b2})]^2\}$$

$$\text{Wald chi-square} = [(0.979 - 0.662)]^2 / \{[0.237]^2 + [0.144]^2\} = 1.306664$$

p value calculated from Wald chi-square (1 degree of freedom) = 0.25299

In the influenza logistic regression model, education was a confounding factor on influenza immunization rates in Mississippi, but not Hawaiʻi. As Table 24 illustrates, graduating from college in Mississippi OR=0.638 (95% CI 0.517 - 0.786); p < 0.001 or some college in Mississippi 0.720 (CI 0.581 - 0.892); p=0.003 impacted influenza immunization rates, but did not impact influenza immunization rates in Hawaiʻi – graduating from college OR=0.864 (95% CI 0.697 - 1.071); p=0.182 or some college OR 1.013 (95% CI 0.832 - 1.233); p=0.901. See Table 24.

Table 24: Impact of Education on Influenza Immunization – Logistic Regression

Influenza Immunization in the Past 12 months.				Odds Ratio	p value
Hawai'i	High School or less vs. College Graduate or more	95% Confidence Interval	Estimate	0.864	0.182
			Lower	0.697	
			Upper	1.071	
Hawai'i	Some College vs. College Graduate or more	95% Confidence Interval	Estimate	1.013	0.901
			Lower	0.832	
			Upper	1.233	
Mississippi	High School or less vs. College Graduate or more	95% Confidence Interval	Estimate	0.638	< 0.001
			Lower	0.517	
			Upper	0.786	
Mississippi	Some College vs. College Graduate or more	95% Confidence Interval	Estimate	0.720	0.003
			Lower	0.581	
			Upper	0.892	

Dependent Variable: DELAY IN CARE DUE TO COSTS (referent category = no)
Model: (Intercept) Health Plan=yes, Marital Status=married, Gender=male, Age=imputed, Income=$50,000 or more, Employed=working, Education=college graduate, Race=white, non-Hispanic

Age, marital status, employment, gender, and income were not found to be significant confounding factors in the multivariate logistic regression analysis for influenza immunization rates. Asians and multi-racial residents were more likely than whites to receive influenza immunizations in Hawai'i OR=1.521 (95% CI 1.232 - 1.878); p < 0.001 and OR=1.392 (95% CI 1.118 - 1.733); P=0.003 respectively, but race was otherwise not confounding in either state relative to influenza immunizations.

The composite results for the logistic regression models are framed in Table 25 for Hawai'i on page 43 and Table 26 for Mississippi on page 44.

Chapter 5 follows on page 45.

Table 25: Composite Logistic Regression Model Results - Hawai'i		
Confounding factors or Variables	Delay in Care due to Costs OR (95% CI)	Flu Shot past 12 Months OR (95% CI)
Have Health Insurance	8.093 (5.24, 12.51)*	0.376 (0.24, 0.59)*
Marital Status		
Divorced	1.433 (0.95, 2.17)	0.910 (0.69, 1.19)
Widowed	0.784 (0.38, 1.62)	1.118 (0.69, 1.82)
Separated	0.670 (0.23, 1.93)	0.619 (0.32, 1.21)
Never Married	1.118 (0.72, 1.75)	0.892 (0.70, 1.14)
Unmarried couple	1.928 (0.88, 4.24)	0.370 (0.22, 0.63)
Gender		
Female v. Male	1.266 (0.91, 1.76)	1.180 (0.99, 1.40)
Imputed Age (years)		
25 to 34 v. 18 to 24	1.752 (0.89, 3.44)	0.923 (0.62, 1.37)
35 to 44 v. 18 to 24	1.423 (0.75, 2.70)	0.964 (0.65, 1.43)
45 to 54 v. 18 to 24	2.320 (1.24, 4.33)*	1.336 (0.91, 1.95)
55 to 64 v. 18 to 24	1.080 (0.56, 2.07)	2.168 (1.47, 3.19)*
Income		
< $15,000	5.474 (3.01, 9.94)*	0.874 (0.55, 1.38)
$15,000 to < $25,000	3.275 (1.97, 5.44)*	0.944 (0.69, 1.30)
$25,000 to < $35,000	1.933 (1.14, 3.26)*	1.142 (0.86, 1.52)
$35,000 to < $50,000	2.094 (1.31, 3.35)*	1.121 (0.88, 1.43)
Unemployed	1.47 (0.72, 3.01)	1.451 (0.89, 2.36)
Education		
High School or Less	1.404 (0.94, 2.10)	0.865 (0.70, 1.07)
Some College	1.196 (0.79, 1.80)	1.013 (0.83, 1.23)
Race		
Asian	0.817 (0.54, 1.25)	1.521 (1.23, 1.88)*
Native Hawai'ian	1.213 (0.44, 3.01)	1.750 (0.99, 3.07)
Multiracial	0.968 (0.66, 1.43)	1.392 (1.12, 1.73)*
Hispanic	1.154 (0.67, 1.99)	1.332 (0.96, 1.85)
Other or missing	1.721 (0.59, 4.99)	2.148 (1.19, 3.89)*

*$p < 0.05$

Table 26: Composite Logistic Regression Model Results - Mississippi		
Confounding factors or Variables	Delay in Care due to Costs OR (95% CI)	Flu Shot past 12 Months OR (95% CI)
Have Health Insurance	3.221 (2.49, 4.17)*	0.516 (0.39, 0.68)*
Marital Status		
Divorced	1.116 (0.86, 1.46)	0.974 (0.77, 1.23)
Widowed	1.206 (0.76, 1.92)	1.082 (0.78, 1.50)
Separated	1.903 (1.24, 2.92)*	1.238 (0.79, 1.95)
Never Married	0.814 (0.59, 1.11)	0.790 (0.59, 1.07)
Unmarried couple		
Gender		
Female v, Male	1.619 (1.26, 2.08)*	0.896 (0.75, 1.07)
Imputed Age (years)		
25 to 34 v. 18 to 24	0.899 (0.56, 1.44)	0.650 (0.43, 0.98)*
35 to 44 v. 18 to 24	1.072 (0.67, 1.71)	0.617 (0.41, 0.93)*
45 to 54 v. 18 to 24	1.166 (0.73, 1.87)	0.814 (0.54. 1.23)
55 to 64 v. 18 to 24	0.836 (0.52, 1.35)	1.557 (1.04, 2.34)
Income		
< $15,000	6.647 (4.47, 9.88)*	0.993 (0.69, 1.43)
$15,000 to < $25,000	5.105 (3.56, 7.33)*	0.849 (0.62, 1.16)
$25,000 to < $35,000	3.697 (2.49, 5.49)*	0.735 (0.54, 1.00)
$35,000 to < $50,000	2.658 (1.85, 3.83)*	0.895 (0.70, 1.14)
Unemployed	0.923 (0.66, 1.30)	0.717 (0.47, 1.10)
Education		
High School or Less	1.421 (1.08, 1.87)*	0.638 (0.52, 0.79)*
Some College	1.410 (1.03, 1.93)*	0.720 (0.58, 0.89)*
Race		
Black	1.024 (0.79, 1.32)	0.873 (0.71, 1.08)
Hispanic	0.581 (0.24, 1.38)	2.030 (1.01, 4.07)*
Multiracial	0.812 (0.40, 1.66)	1.024 (0.50, 2.10)
Other or missing	1.003 (0.54, 1.88)	1.384 (0.77, 2.49)

*$p < 0.05$

Chapter 5 – DISCUSSION

This dissertation compared, contrasted and analyzed healthcare insurance status in Hawai'i and Mississippi and tested the hypothesis that health insurance prevalence improves access to care and health outcomes. It aimed to recommend public health policies and initiatives that promote health insurance prevalence and health insurance plan characteristics that work to improve health outcomes state by state and nationally.

Bivariate analysis supported the precept that health insurance prevalence significantly impacts critical healthcare measures and demonstrated that high performance outcomes indicators like delay in care due to costs, time since last medical check-up, identification of a personal health care provider and influenza status in Hawai'i and Mississippi were significantly improved by health insurance coverage. These findings augment and are consistent with the considerable work of other researchers cited in the literature review in Chapter 2.

Moreover, multivariate logistic regression analysis supported the hypothesis that increased health insurance prevalence in Hawai'i compared to Mississippi improved health access (delay in care due to costs) in Hawai'i to a greater degree than Mississippi. This was significant at $p = 0.000036$.

To recapitulate, nearly 93% of Hawai'ians have health insurance coverage, compared to just 77% of Mississippians significant at $p < 0.001$. Several policy distinctions at the state level work in aggregate to create this difference. For instance, Hawai'i legislated state mandated employer based health insurance for all full-time employees (20 or more hours/week) in 1974. Mississippi does not have state mandated employer based health insurance. Public (government) employees in Hawai'i pay a rate of 3.6% of median income for family health insurance coverage, while Mississippi public employees pay at a rate of 16.6% of median income for comparable family coverage, making health insurance for families less affordable and less available in Mississippi. According to the Kaiser Family Foundation (2009), working parents are eligible for Medicaid at incomes of 100% of the Federal Poverty Level (FPL) in Hawai'i versus 46% of the FPL in Mississippi. Infants, children aged 1 to 5 and children aged 6 to 19 are covered at incomes of 300% of the FPL in Hawai'i; in Mississippi income eligibility for infants, children aged 1 to 5 and children aged 6 to 19 at incomes of 185%, 133% and 100% of the Federal Poverty Level respectively. The FPL income for a family of three in 2007 was $17,170 in Mississippi and $19,750 in Hawai'i (HHS, 2009). In other words, children and parents of children in Mississippi must live at or near dire poverty to be eligible for healthcare benefits under Medicaid.

5.1 Strengths

This research utilized secondary data extracted from the Behavioral Risk Factor Surveillance System. The BRFSS survey data was selected for this study based on its refined methodology, acknowledged validity, and acceptance among policy makers, healthcare academics and public health advocates as a tool to analyze and track health outcomes. Its ready availability in the public domain makes it a particular useful healthcare research data base.

Bivariate methods analyzed the independent and dependent variables. Multivariate regression models further refined the analysis and were constructed around two critical dimensions of healthcare – access (delay in care due to cost of care) and a public health dimension (influenza immunization rates). The multivariate analysis supported the bivariate analysis that health insurance status impacts health outcomes; delay in care due to costs (access to care) was directly and proportionately improved by health insurance prevalence – despite confounding factors like age, race, gender, education, employment and marital status. Logistic regression analysis supported the hypothesis that the prevalence of health insurance in Hawai'i compared to Mississippi significantly improved access to care (delay in care due to costs) in Hawai'i compared to Mississippi. This analytic approach and these findings have significant public health implications and are applicable to legislative decision making as well as health policy initiatives.

Coupled with a qualitative description of federal and state policies regarding health insurance characteristics in Chapter 1, this dissertation exposed specific differences in healthcare policy between Hawai'i and Mississippi that work to improve health insurance status in Hawai'i, accounting for consistently U.S. best or near best health outcomes for Hawai'i and consistently U.S. worst or near worst health outcomes for Mississippi.

5.2 Limitations

Although several methodological features of the Behavioral Risk Factor Surveillance System enhance its validity, the BRFSS is limited to those households with telephones. According to the BRFSS (2007) "people living in the South, minorities, and those in lower socioeconomic groups typically have lower telephone coverage" which describes Mississippi. However, the BRFSS utilized post-stratification weights to mitigate bias for differences in household telephone prevalence in 2007 (BRFSS, 2007).

Even though the BRFSS stands as a highly regarded, time tested, valid survey instrument, the 2007 BRFSS "core" component failed to account in totality for the social determinants of health (Wilkinson and Marmot, 2003). While the 2007 BRFSS did query for social determinants like stress, telephone service, addiction (tobacco and alcohol), healthy food, social and emotional support, and employment, the core component neglected to query issues related to work safety, employment security, job satisfaction, safe housing, transportation, social exclusion and factors related to early life. The magnitude of BRFSS inattention to the social determinants is illustrated by Fossett (1992) who demonstrated that disparities in telecommunication, transportation, neighborhood boundaries, fragile social support, and availability of pediatricians and family physicians in socially divided neighborhoods limited Medicaid's value as a health outcomes lever. The author concluded "Medicaid eligibility, particularly if coupled with increases in Medicaid reimbursement, will improve accessibility of care of newly eligible, near poor children but will have little effect on the availability of care for poor, sicker inner city children" (Fossett, 1992).

The data did not support the hypothesis that increased prevalence of health insurance in Hawai'i compared to Mississippi improved influenza immunizations rates in Hawai'i compared to Mississippi. Influenza immunization rates in Hawai'i were similar to influenza immunization rates in Mississippi. The failure to support the hypothesis can be explained by differences in public health policies. Many departments of public health throughout the U.S. fund immunization initiatives, making insurance status less a determinant for statewide immunization status. Childhood immunization rates lend support to this speculation – Hawai'i ranked 4th in childhood immunization rates at 87.8% in 2008, Mississippi ranked 34 at 78.7% (UHF, 2008) Furthermore, in 2008 Hawai'i ranked 1st in public health funding at $198 per capita; Mississippi ranked 46th at $61 per capita.

Finally, the quantitative analysis in this paper was limited to the responses of persons aged 19 through 64.

5.3 Conclusions

Many of the conclusions in this treatise are drawn from quantitative analysis of the question "Do you have any kind of health care coverage, including health insurance, prepaid

49

plans such as HMOs, or government plans such as Medicare?" which, in the U.S., is but one important factor assuring access to quality healthcare services. It discussed, but did not analyze, the issues surrounding depth and breadth of insurance plans in the U.S. to include health insurance plan limitations on essential services like evidence based health surveillance for procedures like mammography, lipid screening, and colonoscopy not to mention dental and vision care.

In the U.S., if you have examined one health insurance plan, you have examined but one health insurance plan. Private and public plans vary widely jurisdiction to jurisdiction; insurance policy deductions and exclusions modify (limit) coverage; means testing for public plans intimidates (and excludes) eligible recipients; and the federal government has failed to establish (enforce) health insurance plan standards that ensure coverage for essential healthcare services.

An analysis of health insurance plan characteristics and their impact on health outcomes is far beyond the scope of this treatise. To assert that improving health insurance prevalence is the sole solution to state and national healthcare underperformance in U.S. states and the United States, misinterprets and understates the extent of the dilemma.

This analysis of healthcare insurance prevalence supports the conclusions of many other investigators who have shown that access to care is central to high performing healthcare systems. It also made the case that health insurance status has two dimensions – existence (possession) of coverage and extent (breadth and depth) of coverage and that health outcomes measured against health insurance are dependent on both. Indeed, health outcomes in the U.S. could in part be defined by the following formula:

Health Outcomes = Health Insurance Prevalence + Health Insurance Plan Characteristics

In the U.S., the question can be asked, "What good is health insurance, if it denies coverage for preexisting cardiovascular disease or excludes benefit for mammography due to a personal history of breast cancer?" And many would argue that the realm of health insurance in the U.S. is dominated by for profit corporations accountable more to the bottom line than high performance health outcomes.

5.4 Public Health Impact

U.S. health outcomes are dependent on the sum of its parts, i.e. U.S. health outcomes are reliant on the aggregate health outcomes of its 50 states. Yet the federal government has failed to mandate health insurance standards that ensure coverage for essential healthcare services and is loath to adopt universal coverage for all its citizens. In the literature review, this author quoted the work of several respected investigators and reliable sources pointing to the underperformance of U.S. health outcomes compared to many countries worldwide. In particular, it cited The Commonwealth Fund study (Davis, 2007) which concluded three features distinguish healthcare underperformance in the U.S. compared to five other developed countries: 1) lack of universal health insurance coverage, 2) limited adoption of health information technology and 3) marginal utilization of nurse case managers to coordinate the care of chronically ill. This treatise supports Davis' assertion that U.S. underperformance is tied to the dimension of universal health insurance coverage. Furthermore, it contends that short willful application of uniform, universal federal health insurance standards in every state, the United States will continue to lag developed countries worldwide. The American Public Health Association (2009) recently declared its support for healthcare reform and access to affordable and high-quality healthcare in the U.S. "Health reform must strengthen the health service delivery system to ensure access to timely, appropriate, culturally competent and affordable high quality health care services, and create an equitable distribution of resources nationwide." For the United States, the public health implications of the conclusions and recommendations in this manuscript are considerable.

Chapter 6 – RECOMMENDATIONS

As U.S. states and the United States wrestle with healthcare reform, leaders should consider the many factors discussed in this paper. Recommendations include 1) revising the BRFSS to facilitate thorough analysis of the social determinants of health, 2) analyzing the impact/benefit of state mandated employer based health insurance, 3) devising federal regulations and standards that provide universal health plan coverage for essential services and 4) utilizing analytic models similar to this dissertation to craft healthy public policy..

6.1 Revising the BRFSS to permit thorough analysis of the social determinants of health

Two studies not previously referenced point to the critical importance of analyzing the social determinants of health. Flores (1998) studied barriers to healthcare in Latino children concluding that language barrier (11%), transportation (21%), costs (18%), lack of health insurance or no insurance (16%) and wait times (17%) constituted the greatest barriers. Ahmed (2000) conducted a qualitative analysis of the barriers to healthcare access in non-elderly urban poor and identified costs, transportation and telecommunications as significant roadblocks to healthcare services. "The demographic variable that had the greatest number of significant relationships with perceived healthcare barriers was telephone ownership. Respondents who did not have telephones were more likely to report multiple barriers," (Ahmed, 2000).

These studies, and results of other research presented in this treatise, make a strong case for broad inclusion of the social determinants of health by the Centers for Disease Control and Prevention in future iterations of the "core" component of the BRFSS to better identify and understand health outcome drivers in U.S. states.

6.2 Analyzing the impact/benefit of state mandated employer based health insurance

Although state mandated employer based health insurance improves health insurance prevalence in Hawai'i and Massachusetts, U.S. corporations generally hold mandated employer based health insurance in disdain. An exception is Wal-Mart Stores, Inc. one of the nation's largest employers, which recently broke rank. In a letter signed by Wal-Mart CEO Mike Duke, Andrew Stern, president of the Service Employees International Union and John Podesta chief of the Center for American Progress, Wal-Mart declared its support for mandated employer based insurance (Adamy, 2009). Neil Trautwein, vice president of the National Retail Federation (NRF) responded in disgust, illustrating the divisive flavor of healthcare reform in the U.S. "We are surprised and disappointed by Wal-Mart's choice to embrace an employer mandate… we have been one of the foremost opponents''(Adamy, 2009).

Massachusetts instituted employer mandated health coverage in 2006 (Geisel, 2009). In 2008, the Massachusetts Division of Health Care Finance and Policy reported "that 97% of employers provided the required coverage", bringing Massachusetts to near universal coverage statewide (Geisel, 2009). This statistic, coupled with the state's high performance health outcomes – ranked 10th in 2007 improving to 2nd in 2008 (United Health Foundation, 2008) aligns with The Commonwealth Fund declaration that lack of universal coverage is one reason the U.S. underperforms other developed countries in health outcomes.

Despite corporate pushback, federal and state governments must critically evaluate the Hawai'i and Massachusetts models of state mandated employer based insurance to improve health insurance status, access to care and improved health outcomes.

6.3 Devising federal regulations and standards that provide health plan coverage for essential healthcare services

Federal and state health insurance regulatory agencies act to oversee violations of insurance fraud and abuse performing a consumer protection function. Historically federal and state governments have been loath to set minimum standards for health plan coverage. This author asserts the U.S. federal government should appoint a select commission of experts from the United States Preventive Services Task Force, the National Institutes of Health, the Centers for Medicare and Medicaid Services and the Centers for Disease Control and Prevention (CDC) to study and recommend evidence based, health outcomes driven health insurance standards to which all private and public insurers must comply.

6.4 Utilizing analytic models similar to this dissertation to craft public policy

This dissertation devised a bivariate and multivariate analysis of a valid, time tested, and academically respected nationwide telephone survey – the Behavioral Risk Factor Surveillance System (BRFSS) – to demonstrate that health insurance prevalence impacts health outcomes. The BRFSS is available without cost in the public domain. Statistical analysis was performed using SPSS, a respected, readily available bio-statistical software tool. In other words, the research methodology employed in this dissertation, the BRFSS survey instrument and the SPSS statistical package combine to make this research an analytic model for investigations applicable to legislative initiatives that could result in evidence based public health policy leading to improved state and national health outcomes. The data presented in this treatise support the necessity for such strategies.

Word count for dissertation – 10,998

REFERENCES:

Adamy, J., 2009. Wal-Mart backs drive to make companies pay for health coverage. *The Wall Street Journal,* [Online] Available at: http://online.wsj.com/article/SB124640564559176649.html [Accessed 31 October 2009].

Ahmed, S., 2001. Barriers to healthcare access in a non-elderly urban poor American population. *Health and Social Care in the Community,* 9(6), pp 445-453.

American Public Health Association, 2009. APHA 2009 agenda for health reform. [Online] Available at: http://www.apha.org/NR/rdonlyres/681AD0D2-7DD0-48DD-8D59-E425E271156D/0/HlthReform09C6.pdf [Accessed 22 February 2010].

Andrulis, D., 1998. Access to care is the centerpiece in the elimination of socioeconomic disparities in health. *Ann Intern Med,* 129: pp.412-416.

Baldock, J., Manning, N., & Vickerstaff, S. eds., 2007. *Social policy.* Oxford University Press.

Berk, M., 1998. Access to care: How much difference does Medicaid make? *Health Affairs,* 17(3), pp. 169-180.

Bindman, A., 1995. Preventable hospitalizations and access to health care. *JAMA,* 274(22), pp. 305-311.

Buchmueller, T., 2009. The effect of an employer health insurance mandate on health insurance coverage and the demand for labor: evidence from Hawai'i , *Institute for the Study of Labor,* [Online] Available at: http://ideas.repec.org/p/iza/izadps/dp4152.html [Accessed 31 October 2009].

Cantor, J., 2007. Aiming higher: results from a state scorecard on health system performance. *The Commonwealth Fund,* 2007 ed. [Online] Available at: http://www.commonwealthfund.org/Content/Publications/Fund-Reports/2007/Jun/Aiming-Higher--Results-from-a-State-Scorecard-on-Health-System-Performance.aspx [Accessed 17 October 2009].

Centers for Disease Control and Prevention, 2007. Behavioral risk factor surveillance system, [Online] Available at: http://www.cdc.gov/BRFSS/index.htm [Accessed 25 October 2009].

Centers for Disease Control and Prevention, 2007. Behavioral Risk Factor Surveillance System: 2007 Codebook Report. [Online] Available at: http://www.cdc.gov/brfss/technical_infodata/surveydata/2007.htm [Accessed 25 October 2009].

Centers for Disease Control and Prevention, 2007. Behavioral Risk Factor Surveillance System 2007 Questionnaire. [Online] Available at: http://www.cdc.gov/brfss/questionnaires/pdf-ques/2007brfss.pdf [Accessed 14 January 2010].

Centers for Disease Control and Prevention, 2010. Bringing CDC to Congress and Washington. [Online] Available at: http://www.cdc.gov/washington/ [Accessed 22 January 2010].

CNN Money, 2009. Fortune 500 – Our ranking of America's largest corporations. [Online] Available at: http://money.cnn.com/magazines/fortune/fortune500/2009/industries/223/index.html [Accessed 22 March 2010].

Davis, K., 2007. Mirror, mirror on the wall: an international update on the comparative performance of American health care. *The Commonwealth Fund*, [Online]. 59, pp.1-30, Available at: http://www.commonwealthfund.org/Content/Publications/Fund-Reports/2007/May/Mirror--Mirror-on-the-Wall--An-International-Update-on-the-Comparative-Performance-of-American-Healt.aspx [Accessed 19 October 2009].

Employee Benefits Security Administration, 2009. About the employee benefits security administration. U.S. Department of Labor. [Online] Available at: http://www.dol.gov/ebsa/aboutebsa/main.html [Accessed 19 November 2009].

Fahrenthold, D., 2006. Massachusetts bill requires health coverage. *The Washington Post*. [Online] Available at: http://www.washingtonpost.com/wp-dyn/content/article/2006/04/04/AR2006040401937.html [Accessed 22 March 2010].

Flores, G., 1998. Access barriers to health care for Latino children. *Arch of Pediatr Adolesc Med,* 152: pp.1119-1125.

Fossett, J., 1992. Medicaid and access to child health care in Chicago. *Journal of Health Politics, Policy and Law,* 17(2), pp. 273-298.

Freeman, J., 2008. The causal effect of health insurance on utilization and outcomes in adults: a systematic review of US studies. *Med Care*, 46(10):1023-32.

Geisel, J., 2009. 97% of Mass. employers provide mandated health cover. *Business Insurance.com*, [Online] Available at: http://www.businessinsurance.com/article/20091028/NEWS/910289981 [Accessed 31 October 2009].

Guide to Key Policies and Procedures, Employee Benefits and Services-Mississippi State University. [Online] Available at: http://www.hrm.msstate.edu/benefits/benefitsoverview.html [Accessed 1 November 2009].

Hadley, J., 1991. Comparison of uninsured and privately insured hospital patients: condition of admission, resource use, and outcome. *JAMA,* 265, 3, pp. 374-379.

Harris, G., 2009. In Hawai'i's health system, lessons for lawmakers. *The New York Times,* [Online] Available at: http://www.nytimes.com/2009/10/17/health/policy/17Hawai'i .html [Accessed 31 October 2009].

Hawai'i Department of Commerce and Consumer Affairs: Insurance Division, 2009. About insurance, [Online] Available at: http://hawaii.gov/dcca/ins/about [Accessed 31 October 2009].

Hawai'i Department of Labor and Industrial Relations, 2009. Prepaid health care act, 2007, [Online] Available at: http://hawaii.gov/labor/dcd/aboutphc.shtml [Accessed 31 October 2009].

Hawai'i State Department of Health, 2008. Hawai'i behavioral risk factor surveillance system, *2007.* [Online] Available at: http://hawaii.gov/health/statistics/brfss/brfss/brfss2007/brfss07.html [Accessed 25 October 2009].

Hawaii Employer-Union Health Benefits Trust Fund (EUTF): Reference Guide Plan Year 2010, [Online] Available at: http://www.eutf.hawaii.gov/OE_2010/Active_Reference_Guide_2010.pdf [Accessed 1 November 2009].

Hawaii Employer-Union Health Benefits Trust Fund: Employer/Employee Contributions http://www.commonwealthfund.org/Content/Publications/Fund-Reports/2007/May/Mirror--Mirror-on-the-Wall--An-International-Update-on-the-Comparative-Performance-of-American-Healt.aspx [Accessed 17 October 2009].

Hawaii Employer-Union Health Benefits Trust Fund: Employer/Employee Contributions July 1, 2009 through December 31, 2009. [Online] Available at: http://www.eutf.hawaii.gov/OE_2009/Interim_Rates_eff_7-1-09_to_12-31-09_County_Employees.pdf [Accessed 1 November 2009].

HPN, 2009. Health Plan of Nevada/Sierra Health & Life 2009 Product Prospectus.

Husten, C., 2008. Evaluate America's health status. America's health rankings: a call to action for individuals & their communities, 2008 ed., Editorial Comment. p.90. *United Health Foundation*, [Online]. Available at: http://www.americashealthrankings.org/2008/index.html [Accessed 17 October 2009].

Lavizzo-Mourey, R., 2008. It's time to connect what we know with what we do. America's health rankings: a call to action for individuals & their communities, 2008 ed., Foreword. pp. 2-3. *United Health Foundation*, [Online]. Available at: http://www.americashealthrankings.org/2008/index.html [Accessed 17 October 2009].

Litaker, D., 2003. Managed care penetration, insurance status, and access to health care. *Medical Care*, 41(9), pp.1086-1095.

Litaker, D., 2005. Context and healthcare access. *Medical Care,* 43(6) pp.531-540.

Mississippi Insurance Department, 2009. MID mission & history, [Online] Available at: http://www.mid.state.ms.us/pages/mid_mission_history.aspx#mission [Accessed 31 October 2009].

Mississippi State Department of Health, 2008. Mississippi behavioral risk factor surveillance system report, 2007. [Online] Available at: http://www.msdh.state.ms.us/brfss/brfss2007ar.pdf [Accessed 25 October 2009].

Mississippi State Department of Health, 2009. To promote and protect the health of all Mississippians: services and programs, [Online] Available at: http://www.msdh.state.ms.us/ [Accessed 13 May 2009].

Mondragon, D., 1995. Enactment of mandated health insurance in Hawai'i. *Review of Social Economy*. [Online] Available at: http://www.accessmylibrary.com/article-1G1-17163983/enactment-mandated-health-insurance.html [Accessed 31 October 2009].

Mouradian, W., 2000. Disparities in children's oral health and access to dental care. *JAMA*, 284(20), pp. 2625-2631.

National Association of Insurance Commissioners: NAIC states & jurisdictions. *The Center for Insurance Policy & Research, 2009*, [Online] Available at: http://www.naic.org/state_web_map.htm [Accessed 31 October 2009].

National Institutes of Health, 2010. The Nation's Medical Research Agency. [Online] Available at: http://health.nih.gov/ [Accessed 22 January 2010].

Newacheck, P., 1998. The role of Medicaid in ensuring children's access to care. *JAMA*, 280(20), pp. 1789-1793.

Nolte, E., 2003. Measuring the health of nations: analysis of mortality amenable to health care *BMJ*,327:1129. [Online] Available at: http://www.bmj.com/cgi/content/full/327/7424/1129 [Accessed 30 October 2009].

Qureshi, M., 2000. Differences in breast cancer screening rates: an issue of ethnicity or socioeconomics? *Journal of Women's Health & Gender-Based Medicine*, 9(9), pp. 1025-1032.

Shi, L., 1994. Primary care, specialty care, and life chances. *International Journal of Health Services*, 24(3) pp.431-458.

Sox, C., 1998. Insurance or a regular physician: which is the most powerful predictor of health care? *American Journal of Public Health,* 88 (3), 364-370.

The Henry J. Kaiser Family Foundation (KFF), 2009. *Medicaid a Primer, 2009.* [Online] Available at: http://www.kff.org/medicaid/upload/7334-03.pdf [Accessed 5 November 2009].

The Henry J. Kaiser Family Foundation (KFF), 2009. Medicaid state health facts, [Online] Available at: http://www.kaisernetwork.org/gsaresults/search?site=KFForgnopdfs&filter=0&output=xml_no_dtd&client=kff&sp=kff&getfields=*&q=state%20health%20facts&no_pdf=1 [Accessed 13 May 2009].

The Henry J. Kaiser Family Foundation (KFF), 2009. State Health Facts, [Online] Available at: http://www.statehealthfacts.org/comparetable.jsp?ind=130&cat=3 [Accessed 31 October 2009].

The Henry J. Kaiser Family Foundation (KFF), 2009. State Health Facts, What a Family of Four Would Need to Earn in Selected Urban Areas to Have Purchasing Power Equal to 300% of the U.S. Federal Poverty Level ($63,600) 2008, [Online] Available at: http://www.statehealthfacts.org/comparetable.jsp?ind=600&cat=1 [Accessed 1 November 2009].

The Henry J. Kaiser Family Foundation (KFF), 2009. State Health Facts, Median Annual Household Income, 2006-2008, [Online] Available at: http://www.statehealthfacts.org/comparemaptable.jsp?ind=15&cat=1 [Accessed 1 November 2009].

U.S. Census Bureau, 2009. Income, Poverty, and Health Insurance Coverage in the United States: 2008. [Online] Available at: http://www.census.gov/hhes/www/hlthins/hlthin08.html [Accessed 22 March 2010].

U.S. Department of Health & Human Services, 2010. Centers for Medicare and Medicaid Services. [Online] Available at: http://www.cms.hhs.gov/ [Accessed 22 January 2010].

U.S. Department of Health & Human Services, 2009. Medicaid eligibility. *Centers for Medicare and Medicaid Services*, [Online] Available at: http://www.cms.hhs.gov/medicaideligibility/ [Accessed 07 June 2009].

U.S. Department of Health & Human Services, 2009. The 2007 HHS poverty guidelines. *Health and Human Services.* [Online] Available at: http://aspe.hhs.gov/POVERTY/07poverty.shtml [Accessed 17 January 2010].

United Health Foundation (UHF), 2008. America's health rankings: a call to action for individuals & their communities, [Online] 2008, pp. 1-90. Available at: http://www.americashealthrankings.org/2008/index.html [Accessed 17 October 2009].

United States Census Bureau, 2008. State and County QuickFacts, Hawai'i. [Online] Available at: http://quickfacts.census.gov/qfd/states/15000.html [Accessed 28 December 2009].

United States Census Bureau, 2008. State and County QuickFacts, Mississippi. [Online] Available at: http://quickfacts.census.gov/qfd/states/28000.html [Accessed 28 December 2009].

United States Department of Labor, 2009. Employment benefits security administration, [Online] Available at: http://www.dol.gov/ebsa/ [Accessed 31 October 2009].

United States Department of Labor, Employment Benefits Security Administration, 2007. Health benefits coverage under the law, [Online] Available at: http://www.dol.gov/ebsa/pdf/cagtableofcontents.pdf [Accessed 31 October 2009].

United States Preventive Services Task Force, 2010. Recommendations. *Agency for Healthcare Research and Quality*. [Online] Available at: http://www.ahrq.gov/CLINIC/uspstfix.htm#Recommendations [Accessed 23 January 2010].

Wilkinson, R. & Marmot, M. eds., 2003. *The Solid Facts: Social determinants of health*. World Health Organization Europe, 2nd ed. [Online] Available at: http://books.google.com/books?hl=en&lr=&id=QDFzqNZZHLMC&oi=fnd&pg=PP7&dq=%22 Wilkinson%22+%22Social+determinants+of+health:+the+solid+facts%22+&ots=xStHhHSJlu& sig=Zf4VZW9lhbWlBGUIo7jL8IY0V2o#v=onepage&q=&f=false [Accessed 12 January 2010].

World Health Organization, 2008. World Health Statistics, [Online] Available at: http://www.who.int/whosis/whostat/EN_WHS08_Full.pdf [Accessed 20 October 2009].

Weinick, R., 2000. Racial and ethnic differences in access to and use of health care services, 1977 to 1996. *Medical Care Research and Review*, 57(Supplement 1), pp. 36-54.

Weissman, J., 1991. Delayed access to health care: risk factors, reasons, and consequences. *Annals of Internal Medicine*, 114(4) pp. 325-331.

The University of Liverpool/Laureate Online MPH Program
James G. Lenhart, MD
August 28, 2009

Title

An Analysis of the Impact of Healthcare Insurance Availability on Health Outcomes in Hawai'i and Mississippi

Introduction and Background

The availability of healthcare insurance in the United States varies widely from jurisdiction to jurisdiction. State policy, employment/unemployment, eligibility requirements, means testing, poverty, disability, age, gender and others, factor significantly, *and differently*, from state to state. For example, a federal program called Medicaid insures pregnant women during pregnancy and childbirth in most states, but coverage for women of reproductive age may terminate following the post-partum period in some locales. Some states have employer mandated health insurance programs, others do not. Most jurisdictions provide insurance for children through Medicaid, but the extent and duration of coverage may vary state to state. Medicare, a federally sponsored health insurance program for senior citizens (those aged >65 years), provides health benefits for the "elderly", however, forty-seven million *working* Americans ages 18 to 65 went without health insurance in 2007! Several studies have demonstrated the impact of healthcare access on health outcomes. This investigation will compare, contrast and analyze the impact of healthcare insurance availability on health outcomes in Hawai'i and Mississippi. If significant differences in outcomes are identified, recommendations for policy changes to improve the availability of healthcare insurance will be suggested.

Literature Summary

Several sentinel studies set the foundation for this investigation. Davis (2007) compared the health outcomes of the US with five developed countries. She concluded that lack of universal healthcare coverage distinguished US under performance compared to other countries. Cantor (2007) reporting on measures of access, quality, costs, and equity, ranked Hawai'i the best performing and Mississippi the worst performing state. The United Health Foundation (UHF) published America's Health Rankings (2008), which support Cantor's findings. The work of Weinick (2000), Flores (1998), Andrulis (1998), Litaker (2003), Bindman (1995), Weissman (1991), Shi (1994), Qureshi (2000), Ahmed (2001), Litaker (2005) and Ormond (2000) support the inextricable connection between healthcare access and health outcomes. Investigations conducted by Mouradian (2000), Berk (1998), Newacheck (1998) and Fossett (1992) support the importance of Medicaid in improving healthcare access to vulnerable populations. Understanding the impact of healthcare insurance availability on health outcomes can assist state and federal leaders in advocating for policies that improve healthcare insurance availability.

Research Question

What impact does healthcare insurance availability have on health outcomes in the states of Hawai'i and Mississippi?

Study Aims

1. To determine the impact of healthcare insurance availability on healthcare outcomes in Hawai'i and Mississippi

2. To recommend healthcare insurance regulations that improve healthcare insurance availability

Study Objectives
1. To compare, contrast and analyze the impact of healthcare insurance availability on health outcomes in Hawai'i and Mississippi.

Assumptions/Epistemology
This study takes a positivist approach assuming that statistical analysis of healthcare insurance availability and individual health outcomes predicts the overall health of populations.

Methods
This is a quantitative analysis centered on data extracted from the Behavioral Risk Factor Surveillance System (BRFSS) reports published by the Health Department of Hawai'i *Healthy People-Healthy Communities-Healthy Islands,* 2007 and the Mississippi State Department of Health, *To Promote and Protect the Health of all Mississippians,* 2007. In this study, self-reported health insurance status in the states of Hawai'i and Mississippi will be collected, compared and analyzed against the self-reported prevalence of asthma, identification of a medical home, perceived health status, and immunization rates in Hawai'i and Mississippi. Data will be analyzed in SPSS utilizing chi-square to test for statistical significance. Univariate associations significant at $P < .05$ will be further assessed with multivariate analysis of variables and logistic regression models. The following distinction amongst variables is presented for clarity:

- Independent variables – health insurance status
- Dependent variables – prevalence of asthma, identification of a medical home, perceived health status, and immunization rates
- Confounding variables – age, gender, income, and education

Ethics
This research does not involve the NHS or direct engagement with human subjects. Information drawn from the Behavioral Risk Factor Surveillance System (BRFSS) is in the public domain and comprises the raw data sets analyzed in this study.

Research Outcomes
This research proposes to establish the impact of healthcare insurance availability on health outcomes in Hawai'i and Mississippi.

Costs
Supplies - $50 US; Internet Service Provision - $70US; transcription - $100. Total - $220 US.

Proposed Timetable
Research proposal submitted August 31, 2009; ethics application submitted September 8, 2009. BRFSS data entered into SPSS September 15 through September 29, 2009. Introductory chapter submitted October 15, 2009. BRFSS data analyzed & submitted October 29, 2009. Discussion submitted November 23, 2009. Notice to submit draft form December 4, 2009. Submit final draft December 21, 2009; final dissertation submitted January 11, 2009.

Key References:

Ahmed, S., 2001. Barriers to healthcare access in a non-elderly urban poor American population. *Health and Social Care in the Community,* 9(6), pp 445-453.

Andrulis, D., 1998. Access to care is the centerpiece in the elimination of socioeconomic disparities in health. *Annals of Internal Medicine*, 129, pp.412-416.

Baldock, J., Manning, N., & Vickerstaff, S. eds., 2007. *Social Policy.* 3rd ed. Oxford, Oxford University Press.

Berk, M., 1998. Access to care: How much difference does Medicaid make? *Health Affairs,* 17(3), pp. 169-180

Bilton, T., 2002. *Introductory Sociology.* Ch. 13, pp. 359-367. Basingstoke, Palgrave, MacMillan. [Online] Available at: http://www.palgrave.com/bilton/pdfs/0333 945719 14 cha13.pdf [Accessed 14 June 2009].

Bindman, A. 1995 Preventable hospitalizations and access to care. *JAMA*, [Online] 274(22), pp. 305-311. Abstract from PubMed database. Available at: http://www.ncbi.nlm.nih.gov/sites/entrez?orig_db=PubMed&db=pubmed&cmd=Search&TransS chema=title&term=%22JAMA%20%3A%20the%20journal%20of%20the%20American%20Me dical%20Association%22%5BJour%5D%20AND%20274%5Bvolume%5D%20AND%204%5B issue%5D%20AND%20305%5Bpage%5D%20AND%201995%5Bpdat%5D%20AND%20Bind man%20AB%5Bauthor%5D%20AND%20Preventable [Accessed 12 July 2009].

Cantor, J., 2007. Aiming higher: results from a state scorecard on health system performance. *The Commonwealth Fund*, 2007 ed. [Online] Available at: http://www.commonwealthfund.org/Content/Publications/Fund-Reports/2007/Jun/Aiming-Higher--Results-from-a-State-Scorecard-on-Health-System-Performance.aspx [Accessed 13 May 2009].

Davis, K., 2007. Mirror, mirror on the wall: an international update on the comparative performance of American health care. *The Commonwealth Fund*, 2007 ed. [Online] Available at: http://www.commonwealthfund.org/Content/Publications/Fund-Reports/2007/May/Mirror--Mirror-on-the-Wall--An-International-Update-on-the-Comparative-Performance-of-American-Healt.aspx [Accessed 13 May 2009].

Flores, G., 1998. Access barriers to health care for Latino children. *Archives of Pediatric Adolescent Medicine,* 152, pp.1119-1125.

Fossett, J., 1992. Medicaid and access to child health care in Chicago. *Journal of Health Politics, Policy and Law,* 17(2), pp. 273-298.

Freeman, J., 2008. The causal effect of health insurance on utilization and outcomes in adults: a systematic review of US studies. *Med Care*, 46(10):1023-32.

Hawai'i Department of Health, 2009. *Healthy People-Healthy Communities-Healthy Islands,* [Online] Available at: http://hawaii.gov/health/ [Accessed 13 May 2009].

HHS.gov, 2009. *Centers for Medicare and Medicaid Services: Medicaid Eligibility*, [Online] Available at: http://www.cms.hhs.gov/medicaideligibility/ [Accessed 07 June 2009].

Litaker, D., 2003. Managed care penetration, insurance status, and access to health care. *Medical Care*, 41(9), pp.1086-1095.

Litaker, D., 2005. Context and healthcare access. *Medical Care*. 43(6) pp.531-540.

Mississippi State Department of Health, 2009. *To Promote and Protect the Health of all Mississippians,* [Online] Available at: http://www.msdh.state.ms.us/ [Accessed 13 May 2009].

Mouradian, W., 2000. Disparities in children's oral health and access to dental care. *JAMA,* 284(20), pp. 2625-2631.

Newacheck, P., 1998. The role of Medicaid in ensuring children's access to care. *JAMA,* 280(20), pp. 1789-1793.

Ormond, B., 2000. Supporting the Rural Health Care Safety Net. *Urban Institute*, [Online] Available at: http://www.urban.org/url.cfm?ID=309437&renderforprint=1 [Accessed 12 July 2009].

Qureshi, M., 2000. Differences in breast cancer screening rates: an issue of ethnicity or socioeconomics. *Journal of Women's Health & Gender-Based Medicine*, 9(9), pp. 1025-1032.

Shi, L. 1994. Primary care, specialty care, and life chances. *International Journal of Health Services*, 24(3) pp.431-458.

The Henry J. Kaiser Family Foundation, 2009. *Medicaid State Health Facts* [Online] Available at:
http://www.kaisernetwork.org/gsaresults/search?site=KFForgnopdfs&filter=0&output=xml_no_dtd&client=kff&sp=kff&getfields=*&q=state%20health%20facts&no_pdf=1 [Accessed 13 May 2009].

United Health Foundation, 2008. *America's Health Rankings: A Call to Action for Individuals & Their Communities,* 2008 ed. [Online] Available at:
http://www.americashealthrankings.org/2008/index.html [Accessed 13 May 2009].

Weinick, R., 2000. Racial and ethnic differences in access to and use of health care services, 1977 to 1996. *Medical Care Research and Review*, 57(Supplement 1), pp. 36-54.

Weissman, J., 1991. Delayed access to care: risk factors, reasons, and consequences. *Annals of Internal Medicine*, 114(4) pp. 325-331.

APPENDIX 2

ETHICS APPLICATION

UNIVERSITY OF
LIVERPOOL

COMMITTEE ON RESEARCH ETHICS
APPLICATION FOR APPROVAL OF A PROJECT INVOLVING
HUMAN PARTICIPANTS, HUMAN DATA, OR HUMAN MATERIAL

This application form is to be used by researchers seeking approval from the University Committee on Research Ethics or from an approved School or Departmental Research Ethics Committee.

Applications to the University Research Ethics Sub-Committees, with the specified attachments, should be **submitted electronically to** ethics@liv.ac.uk. Applications to an approved School / Departmental Committee should be submitted to their local address, available at http://www.liv.ac.uk/researchethics/deptcommittees.htm.

This form must be completed by following the guidance notes, accessible at
www.liv.ac.uk/researchethics.

Incomplete forms will be returned to the applicant.

BEFORE COMPLETING YOUR APPLICATION PLEASE CONFIRM WHAT APPROVAL YOU ARE SEEKING (please check):

a) Expedited review of an individual research project ☒

b) Full committee review of an individual research project ☐

c) Expedited generic* approval ☐

d) Committee review generic* approval ☐

*to cover a cohort of projects using similar methodologies. Boundaries of the research must be defined clearly. Approval may be granted for up to 5 years and will be subject to annual review.

Office Use Only (for final hard copies)	
Reference Number:	RETH
Date final copy received:	
Approval decision:	
Approved – no conditions	☐
Committee	☐
Chairs Action	☐
Expedited	☐
Approved with conditions	☐
Committee	☐
Chairs Action	☐
Expedited	☐

Declaration of the:

Principal Investigator ☐   **OR**   **Supervisor and Student Investigator** ☒
(please check as appropriate)

- The information in this form is accurate to the best of my knowledge and belief, and I take full responsibility for it.

- I have read and understand the University's Policy on Research Ethics

- I undertake to abide by the ethical principles underlying the Declaration of Helsinki and the University's good practice guidelines on the proper conduct of research, together with the codes of practice laid down by any relevant professional or learned society.

- If the research is approved, I undertake to adhere to the study plan, the terms of the full application of which the REC has given a favourable opinion, and any conditions set out by the REC in giving its favourable opinion.

- I undertake to seek an ethical opinion from the REC before implementing substantial amendments to the study plan or to the terms of the full application of which the REC has given a favourable opinion.

- I understand that I am responsible for monitoring the research at all times.

- If there are any serious adverse events, I understand that I am responsible for immediately stopping the research and alerting the Research Ethics Committee within 24 hours of the occurrence, via ethics@liv.ac.uk.

- I am aware of my responsibility to be up to date and comply with the requirements of the law and relevant guidelines relating to security and confidentiality of personal data.

- I understand that research records/data may be subject to inspection for audit purposes if required in future.

- I understand that personal data about me as a researcher in this application will be held by the University and that this will be managed according to the principles established in the Data Protection Act.

- I understand that the information contained in this application, any supporting documentation and all correspondence with the Research Ethics Committee relating to the application, will be subject to the provisions of the Freedom of Information Acts. The information may be disclosed in response to requests made under the Acts except where statutory exemptions apply.

- I understand that all conditions apply to any co-applicants and researchers involved in the study, and that it is my responsibility to ensure that they abide by them.

  For Supervisors: I understand my responsibilities as supervisor, and will ensure, to the best of my abilities, that the student investigator abides by the University's Policy on Research Ethics at all times.

- **For the Student Investigator**: I understand my responsibilities to work within a set of safety, ethical and other guidelines as agreed in advance with my supervisor and understand that I must comply with the University's regulations and any other applicable code of ethics at all times.

Signature of Principal Investigator ☐   **or**   **Supervisor** ☒:   ....
Date: (04/09/2009)
Print Name: Jill A. Wiseberg
Signature of Student Investigator: ....   **Date:** (04/09/2009)
Print Name: James G. Lenhart

SECTION A - IDENTIFYING INFORMATION

A1)   **Title of the research** (PLEASE INCLUDE A SHORT LAY TITLE IN BRACKETS).

>

A2)   **Principal Investigator** ☐   **OR**   **Supervisor**   ☒ **(please check as appropriate)**

Title:	Professor	Staff number:	
Forename/Initials:	Jill	Surname:	Wiseberg
Post:	Faculty	Department:	Publich Health
Telephone:	1+(561)613-1071	E-mail:	jill.wiseberg@my.ohecampus.com

A3)   **Co-applicants** *(including student investigators)*

Title and Name	Post	Department/ School/Institution if not UoL	Phone	Email
James Lenhart	Student Investigator	MPH Online Programme	702-497-6558	jlenhart2@cox.net

SECTION B - PROJECT DETAILS

B1)   **Proposed study dates and duration**

Start date:	01/09/2009	End date:	12/01/2010

B2)   **Give a full lay summary of the purpose, design and methodology of the planned research.**

Study Aims

1.   To determine the impact of healthcare insurance availability on healthcare outcomes in Hawai'i and Mississippi

2.   To recommend healthcare insurance regulations that improve healthcare insurance availability

Study Objectives

1.   To compare, contrast and analyze the impact of healthcare insurance availability on health outcomes in Hawai'i and Mississippi.

Methods

This is a quantitative analysis centered on data extracted from the Behavioral Risk Factor This is This is a quantitative analysis centered on data extracted from the Behavioral Risk Factor Surveillance System (BRFSS) reports published by the Health Department of Hawai'i Healthy People-Healthy Communities-Healthy Islands, 2007 and the Mississippi State Department of Health, To Promote and Protect the Health of all Mississippians, 2007. In this study, self-reported health insurance status in the states of Hawai'i and Mississippi will be collected, compared and analyzed against the self-reported prevalence of asthma, identification of a medical home, perceived health status, and immunization rates in Hawai'i and Mississippi. Data will be analyzed in SPSS utilizing the chi-square to test for statistical significance. Multivariate associations between variables will be analyzed. The following distinction amongst variables is presented for clarity:

- Independent variables – health insurance status
- Dependent variables – prevalence of asthma, identification of a medical home, perceived health status, and immunization rates
- Confounding variables – age, gender, income, and education

B3) **List any research assistants, sub-contractors or other staff not named above who will be involved in the research and detail their involvement.**

B4) **List below all research sites, and their Lead Investigators, to be included in this study.**

Research Site	Individual Responsible	Position and contact details
The home office of James Lenhart in Las Vegas, NV	James G. Lenhart, MD (MPH student U of Liverpool, Laureate Online)	Student Investigator 10941 Keymar Dr. Las Vegas, NV 89135

B5) **Are the results of the study to be disseminated in the public domain?**
YES ☒   NO ☐
  ➢ *If not, why not?*

B6) **Give details of the funding of the research, including funding organisation(s), amount applied for or secured, duration, and UOL reference**

Funding Body	Amount	Duration	UoL Reference
Personal funds for telephone, supplies, internet service	$120	Project	NA

B7) Give details of any interests, commercial or otherwise, you or your co-applicants have in the funding body.

None

SECTION C - EXPEDITED REVIEW

C1)

a) Will the study involve recruitment of participants outside the UK?	No
b) Does the study involve participants who are particularly vulnerable or unable to give informed consent? *(e.g. children, people with learning or communication disabilities, people in custody, people engaged in illegal activities such as drug-taking, your own students in an educational capacity) (Note: this does not include secondary data authorised for release by the data collector for research purposes.)*	No
c) Will the study require obtaining consent from a "research participant advocate" (for definition see guidance notes) in lieu of participants who are unable to give informed consent? *(e.g. for research involving children or, people with learning or communication disabilities)*	No
d) Will it be necessary for participants, whose consent to participate in the study will be required, to take part without their knowledge at the time? *(e.g. covert observation using photography or video recording)*	No
e) Does the study involve deliberately misleading the participants?	No
f) Will the study require discussion of sensitive topics that may cause distress or embarrassment to the participant or potential risk of disclosure to the researcher of criminal activity or child protection issues? *(e.g. sexual activity, criminal activity)*	No
g) Are drugs, placebos or other substances (e.g. food substances, vitamins) to be administered to the study participants or will the study involve invasive, intrusive or potentially harmful procedures of any kind?	No
h) Will samples (e.g. blood, DNA, tissue) be obtained from participants?	No
i) Is pain or more than mild discomfort likely to result from the study?	No
j) Could the study induce psychological stress or anxiety or cause harm or negative consequences beyond the risks encountered in normal life?	No
k) Will the study involve prolonged or repetitive testing?	No
l) Will financial inducements (other than reasonable expenses and compensation for time) be offered to participants?	No

C2)

a) Will the study seek written, informed consent?	No
b) Will participants be informed that their participation is voluntary?	No
c) Will participants be informed that they are free to withdraw at any time?	No
d) Will participants be informed of aspects relevant to their continued participation in the study?	No
e) Will participants' data remain confidential?	No
f) Will participants be debriefed?	No

If you have answered 'no' to all items in SECTION C1 and 'yes' to all questions in SECTION C2 the application will be processed through expedited review.

If you have answered "Yes" to one or more questions in Section C1, or "No" to one or more questions in Section C2, but wish to apply for expedited review, please make the case below. See research ethics website for an example "case for expedited review".

C3)   **Case for Expedited Review** – *To be used if asking for expedited review despite answering YES to questions in C1 or NO to answers in C2.*

This research does not involve the NHS or direct engagement with any human subjects. Information drawn from the Behavioral Risk Factor Surveillance System (BRFSS) is in the public domain and comprises the entire data analyzed in this study. This is a quantitative analysis centered from data extracted from the Behavioral Risk Factor Surveillance System (BRFSS) reports published by the Health Department of Hawai'i "Healthy People-Healthy Communities-Healthy Islands", 2007 at http://hawaii.gov/health/statistics/brfss/index.html and the Mississippi State Department of Health, "To Promote and Protect the Health of all Mississippians", 2007 at http://www.msdh.state.ms.us/msdhsite/search/index.cfm?criteria=BRFSS

ABOUT BRFSS http://www.cdc.gov/brfss/about.htm
The Behavioral Risk Factor Surveillance System (BRFSS) is a state-based system of health surveys that collects information on health risk behaviors, preventive health practices, and health care access primarily related to chronic disease and injury. For many states, the BRFSS is the only available source of timely, accurate data on health-related behaviors.
BRFSS was established in 1984 by the Centers for Disease Control and Prevention (CDC); currently data are collected monthly in all 50 states, the District of Columbia, Puerto Rico, the U.S. Virgin Islands, and Guam. More than 350,000 adults are interviewed each year, making the BRFSS the largest telephone health survey in the world. States use BRFSS data to identify emerging health problems, establish and track health objectives, and develop and evaluate public health policies and programs. Many states also use BRFSS data to support health-related legislative efforts.

SECTION D - PARTICIPANT DETAILS

D1)   How many participants will be recruited?

> NA

D2)   How was the number of participants decided upon?

> NA

D3)

a)   Describe how potential participants in the study will be identified, approached and recruited.

> NA

b)   Inclusion criteria:

> NA

c)   Exclusion criteria:

> NA

d)   Are any specific groups to be excluded from this study? If so please list them and explain why:

> NA

e)   Give details for cases and controls separately if appropriate:

> NA

f)   Give details of any advertisements:

> NA

D4)   State the numbers of participants from any of the following groups and justify their inclusion

Children under 16 years of age:	NA
Adults with learning disabilities:	NA
Adults with dementia:	NA
Prisoners:	NA
Young Offenders:	NA

Adults who are unable to consent for themselves:	NA
Healthy Volunteers:	NA
Those who could be considered to have a particularly dependent relationship with the investigator, e.g. those in care homes, students of the PI or Co-applicants:	NA
Other vulnerable groups (please list):	NA

D5)

    a)   Describe the arrangements for gaining informed consent from the research participants.

NA

    b)   If participants are to be recruited from any of the potentially vulnerable groups listed above, give details of extra steps taken to assure their protection, including arrangements to obtain consent from a legal, political or other appropriate representative in addition to the consent of the participant *(e.g. HM Prison Service for research with young offenders, Head Teachers for research with children etc.)*.

NA

    c)   If participants might not adequately understand verbal explanations or written information given in English, describe the arrangements for those participants *(e.g. translation, use of interpreters etc.)*

NA

    d)   Where informed consent is not to be obtained (including the deception of participants) please explain why.

NA

D6)   What is the potential for benefit to research participants, if any?

Making recommendations for state healthcare insurance regulations that improve healthcare insurance availability to residents of Hawai'i and Mississippi

D7) State any fees, reimbursements for time and inconvenience, or other forms of compensation that individual research participants may receive. Include direct payments, reimbursement of expenses or any other benefits of taking part in the research?

> NA

SECTION E - RISKS AND THEIR MANAGEMENT

E1) Describe in detail the potential physical or psychological adverse effects, risks or hazards (minimal, moderate, high or severe) of involvement in the research for research participants.

> Minimal risk; disseminated knowledge of the results could have a depressing effect on the residents of Hawai'i and Mississippi

E2) Explain how the potential benefits of the research outweigh any risks to the participants.

> Results of the study could shape heathcare insurance public policy in both states

E3) Describe in detail the potential adverse effects, risks or hazards (minimal, moderate, high or severe) of involvement in the research for the researchers.

> None

E4) Will individual or group interviews/questionnaires discuss any topics or issues that might be sensitive, embarrassing or upsetting, or is it possible that criminal or other disclosures requiring action could take place during the study (e.g. during interviews/group discussions, or use of screening tests for drugs)?

YES ☐   NO ☒
> ➢ *If Yes, give details of procedures in place to deal with these issues.*

> NA

E5) Describe the measures in place in the event of any unexpected outcomes or adverse events to participants arising from their involvement in the project

> NA

E6) **Explain how the conduct of the project will be monitored to ensure that it conforms with the study plan and relevant University policies and guidance.**

> The dissertation advisor and the DOS committee assigned by University of Liverpool and Laureate Online Education will guide and monitor the research project

SECTION F - DATA ACCESS AND STORAGE

F1) **Where the research involves any of the following activities at any stage (including identification of potential research participants), state what measures have been put in place to ensure confidentiality of personal data (e.g. encryption or other anonymisation procedures will be used)**

Electronic transfer of data by magnetic or optical media, e-mail or computer networks	BRFSS data is in the public domain and available at http://hawaii.gov/health/statistics/brfss/index.html and http://www.msdh.state.ms.us/msdhsite/search/index.cfm?criteria=BRFSS
Sharing of data with other organisations	BRFSS data is in the public domain and available at http://hawaii.gov/health/statistics/brfss/index.html and http://www.msdh.state.ms.us/msdhsite/search/index.cfm?criteria=BRFSS
Export of data outside the European Union	NA
Use of personal addresses, postcodes, faxes, e-mails or telephone numbers	NA
Publication of direct quotations from respondents	NA
Publication of data that might allow identification of individuals	NA
Use of audio/visual recording devices	NA
Storage of personal data on any of the following:	
Manual files	NA

Home or other personal computers	Symantic End Point protection
University computers	NA
Private company computers	NA
Laptop computers	NA

F2) **Who will have control of and act as the custodian for the data generated by the study?**

The PI

F3) **Who will have access to the data generated by the study?**

The student investigator (James G. Lenhart, MD)

F4) **For how long will data from the study be stored?**

The BRFSS data is available on the public domain; the analyzed data will be stored for 12 months or less or longer depending on University of Liverpool policies

SECTION G – PEER REVIEW

G1) **Has the project undergone peer review?**

YES ☐   NO ☒

If yes, by whom was this carried out?

SECTION G - CHECKLIST OF ENCLOSURES

Study Plan / Protocol	Yes
Recruitment advertisement	N/A
Participant information sheet	N/A
Participant Consent form	N/A
Research Participant Advocate Consent form	N/A
Evidence of external approvals	N/A
Questionnaires on sensitive topics	N/A
Interview schedule	N/A
Debriefing material	N/A
Other (please specify)	N/A
Evidence of peer review (If G1 = Yes)	Yes

APPENDIX 3

UNIVERSITY of LIVERPOOL DISSERTAION APPROVALS

DISSERTAION PROPOSAL APPROVAL

September 29, 2009

```
-----Original Message-----
From: Susan Jones [mailto:sue.jones@my.ohecampus.com]
Sent: 29 September 2009 14:14
To: James Lenhart
Cc: UKL1.DSTOFF.20080925.208@embanet.com; Jackie Wilson; Jill Wiseberg
Subject: Dissertation Proposal Approved
```

Dear Jim,

I am happy to inform you that your dissertation proposal has been approved.

Please remember that your final submission date is 03 Feb 2010. Your Dissertation Advisor Jill Wiseberg will be there to provide you with advice and guidance, but the responsibility to meet this goal is yours.

On behalf of Laureate Online Education and The University of Liverpool we would like to wish you every success in this challenging part of your studies.

Regards,

Director of Online Studies

StudentID: 15173306

DISSERTATION ETHICS PANEL APPROVAL

Author: Jill Wiseberg (DA)
Posted date: Tuesday, October 20, 2009 12:44:58 PM EDT
Last modified date: Tuesday, October 20, 2009 12:44:58 PM EDT
Total views: 4 **Your views:** 3

‹ Previous Post | Next Post ›

Show Parent Post

Hey Jim -

Good news - you received Ethics Approval from the Panel, so you are good to go!!!

Please let me know if I can assist w/anything.

Jill~

APPENDIX 3 (continued)

APPROVAL FOR EXTENSION OF DEADLINE

February 3, 2010
Hi Jim,
Thanks for your further email. I have now discussed your request with the Director of Online Studies for the MPH programme, Sue Jones, and she has agreed to approve a one-month extension to take account of your confusion. Your new final submission deadline is 28th February 2010. This decision will be formally agreed at the next meeting of the Academic Progress Committee.
Here below is the email you received on 29th September concerning Proposal Approval. It was sent by the Director to your eCampus email account and copied to your DA.
So make the most of these final extra days and all good luck!

Kind regards,

Jackie

Jackie Wilson
Student Support Manager
Laureate Online Education, the
e-learning partner of the University of Liverpool
Laureate Online Education B.V.
De Entree 11-13
1101 BH Amsterdam Z.O.
The Netherlands
t: +31 (0)20 713 0023
f: +31 (0)20 713 0099
e:jackie.wilson@ohecampus.com
jackie_wilson@embanet.com
w:http://www.uol.ohecampus.com

APPENDIX 4

HAWAI'I'S PREPAID HEALTH CARE (PHC) ACT

"Enacted in 1974, the Hawaii PHC Act was the first in the nation to set minimum standards of health care benefits for workers. Employers, excluding Federal, State and City government and other categories specifically excluded by the law (sections **393-3(8)**, **393-5** and **393-6**) are required to provide Hawaii employees, who suffer a disability due to non-work related illness or injury, with adequate medical coverage for non-work related illness or injury, protecting them from the high cost of medical and hospital care.

Employers must provide health care coverage to employees who work at least twenty (20) hours per week and earn 86.67 times the current Hawaii minimum wage a month ($7.25 x 86.67 = $628). Coverage commences after four (4) consecutive weeks of employment or the earliest time thereafter at which coverage can be provided by the health care plan contractor, which is usually the first of the month.

Employers can choose one of the following three ways to provide the mandated coverage to their employees.

- Purchase an **approved plan**. In Hawaii , insurance companies, mutual benefit societies and health maintenance organizations can sell health care plans to Hawaii employers directly. These plans must be reviewed by the PHC Advisory Council and approved by the Director of the Department of Labor and Industrial Relations (DLIR) before they can be marketed to employers.
- Purchase an insured plan of employers' choice. Some employers with corporate officers located outside of Hawaii purchase a health care plan and offer such plan to their employees on a nationwide basis. Employers that choose this option must submit their plan to DLIR for review by the PHC Advisory Council and approval by the Director to ensure the benefits are comparable to plans sold in Hawaii .
- Provide a health care plan that is funded by the employer. As a self-insurer, the employer must show **proof of financial solvency and ability to pay benefits** by furnishing DLIR with the latest audited financial statements for review. Following the initial approval, the audited financial statements must be filed annually for continued approval. Employers choosing this option must complete an application for self-insurance (**Form HC-61**) as well as submit a copy of their health care plan to DLIR for review by the PHC Advisory Council and approval by the Director to ensure the benefits are comparable to plans sold in Hawaii.

All health care plans, whether sold by health care contractors or submitted by employers, must be approved by DLIR as meeting the prescribed minimum standards. Such determination is made by the Director under the advisement of a **seven-member PHC Advisory Council** consisting of representatives from the medical and public health care professions, from consumer interests, and from the prepaid health care protection industry. Upon approval, plans are designated as a 7(a) or 7(b) plan. Plans designated as 7(a) are equal to or better than the benefits offered by the plan with the largest number of subscribers (also known as the prevalent plan) in the State of Hawaii . (**Click here for a summary of benefits offered by the PPO and**

HMO prevalent plans.) Plans designated as 7(b) provide for sound basic hospital, surgical, medical, and other health care benefits; however, plan's benefits, such as, the deductible, out of pocket limit, lifetime maximum benefit, benefit level and copayments, may be more limited than the benefits provided by plans qualifying as 7(a). Plans qualifying as 7(b) require the employer to pay one-half of the cost for dependents' coverage.

Employers may elect to pay the entire monthly premium or share the cost with their employees. Employers must pay at least 50% of the premium cost, but the employees' share cannot exceed the lesser of 50% of the premium cost or 1.5% of the employees' monthly gross earnings. Cost sharing for dependents is determined by plan type. If employers purchase an approved plan, the health care contractor is responsible for informing the employers whether they are responsible for contributing toward dependents' coverage. If employers submit a plan for approval, DLIR is responsible for informing the employers of their plan approval designation and whether they are responsible for contributing toward dependents' coverage.

There are situations where employees can waive the mandated coverage. These include being covered by a federally established health insurance, such as, Medicare and Medicaid, covered as a dependent under a qualified plan, recipient of public assistance and covered by state-legislated health plan, covered under their own personal health insurance policy or a follower of a religious group who depends for healing upon prayer or other spiritual means. Employees are required to complete "Employee Notification to Employer" (**Form HC-5**) every calendar year to validate the exemption so that employers are relieved of the responsibility for providing the mandated health care coverage.

Unless specifically excluded under the law or a Notice to Employer to waive coverage is filed with the employers, all employees who meet the eligibility requirements are entitled to health care coverage through employer-based group policies. Complaints related to non-coverage by employers can be filed with our Investigation Section in Honolulu or on the neighbor-island, the Department of Labor and Industrial Relations District Office nearest the complainant for assistance. Complaints related to benefits of the plan are usually filed directly with the health care contractors who are regulated by the Insurance Division."

Hawai'i Department of Labor and Industrial Relations: Prepaid Health Care Act, 2007. [Online] Available at: http://hawaii.gov/labor/dcd/aboutphc.shtml [Accessed 31 October 2009].

APPENDIX 5
STATE MEDICAID FACT SHEET 2006-2007 - Hawaii and Mississippi

DEMOGRAPHIC PROFILES	HI	MS	HI	MS	Notes
Total Residents	1,235,470	2,889,110	—	—	
Income					
Poor: Below Federal Poverty Level (FPL)	191,600	791,900	15.5	27.4	% of total residents
Near-Poor: 100-199% of the FPL	220,830	597,520	17.9	20.7	% of total residents
Non-Poor: 200% of the FPL and above	823,050	1,499.700	66.6	51.9	% of total residents
Median Annual Income	$63,164	$35,971	—	—	
Age					
Children (0-18)	307,390	823,490	25	28	% of total residents
Poor Children	55,860	303,590	18	37	% of total children
Adults (19-64)	752,750	1,732,250	61	60	% of total residents
Poor Adults	111,440	410,260	15	24	% of total adults
Elderly (65+)	175,330	333,370	14	12	% of total residents
Poor Elderly	24,300	78,050	14	23	% of total elderly
Distribution by Race/Ethnicity					
White	220.100	1,664,150	18	58	% of total residents
Black	24,440	1,071,540	2	37	% of total residents
Hispanic	85,170	69,710	7	2	% of total residents
Other	905,770	83,710	73	3	% of total residents
Non-Citizen	94,220	51,010	8	2	% of total residents
Population Living in Non-Metropolitan Areas	342,590	1,626,550	28	56	% of total residents
HEALTH INSURANCE PROFILES	HI	MS	HI	MS	
Health Insurance Coverage of the Non-elderly					
Medicaid	122,350	478,700	11.5	18.7	% of non-elderly
Children	71,780	302,150	58.7	63.1	% of Medicaid
Adults	50,570	176,560	41.3	36.9	% of Medicaid
Uninsured	100,420	564,340	9.5	22.1	% of non-elderly
Children	17,980	133,780	17.9	23.7	% of uninsured
Adults	82,430	430,560	82.1	76.3	% of uninsured
Poor: Below Federal Poverty Level (FPL)	40,820	312,600	40.6	55.4	% of uninsured
Near-Poor: 100-199% of the FPL	25,050	146,350	24.9	25.9	% of uninsured
Employer Sponsored Insurance	754,330	1,302,960	71.2	51.0	% of non-elderly
Medicaid Enrollment	HI	MS	HI	MS	
Total Enrollment, FY2006	217,300	787,700	—	—	% of total residents
Children	95,000	398,700	43.7	50.6	% of Medicaid enrollees
Adults	74,300	135,400	34.2	17.2	% of Medicaid enrollees
Elderly	23,000	94,800	10.6	12.0	% of Medicaid enrollees
Disabled	25,000	158,800	11.5	20.2	% of Medicaid enrollees
% Enrolled in Managed Care, 2007	—	—	79.9	0.0	% of Medicaid enrollees
Medicaid Eligibility Levels by Annual Income and FPL, 2009	HI	MS	HI	MS	
Working Parents	$20,244	$8,064	100	46	% of federal poverty level
Pregnant Women	$37,444	$32,560	185	185	% of federal poverty level
Infants	$60,720	$32,560	300	185	% of federal poverty level
Children 1-5	$60,720	$23,408	300	133	% of federal poverty level
Children 6-19	$60,720	$17,600	300	100	% of federal poverty level

Adapted from: The Henry J. Kaiser Family Foundation, 2009. *Medicaid State Health Facts* Available at: http://www.kaisernetwork.org/gsaresults/search?site=KFForgnopdfs&filter=0&output=xml_no_dtd&client=kff&sp =kff&getfields=*&q=state%20health%20facts&no_pdf=1

APPENDIX 6
LEXICON of *America's Health Rankings, 2008* HEALTH DETERMINANTS & OUTCOMES

HEALTH DETERMINANTS	DESCRIPTION
Personal Behaviors	
Prevalence of Smoking	Percentage of population over age 18 that smokes on a regular basis. This is an indication of known, addictive, health-adverse behaviors within the population. (www.americashealthrankings.org/2008/smoking.html).
Prevalence of Binge Drinking	Percentage of population over age 18 that has drunken excessively in the last 30 days. Binge drinking is defined as 5 drinks for a male and 4 for a female in one setting. It is a proxy indicator for excessive drug and alcohol use within a population. (www.americashealthrankings.org/2008/binge.html).
Prevalence of Obesity	Percentage of the population estimated to be obese, with a body mass index (BMI) of 30.0 or higher. Obesity is known to contribute to a variety of diseases, including heart disease, diabetes, and general poor health. (www.americashealthranking.org/2008/obesity.html).
Community & Environment	
High School Graduation	Percentage of incoming ninth graders who graduate in four years from a high school with a regular degree, as reported by NCES in compliance with the No Child Left Behind initiative. It is an indication of the individual's ability to learn about, create and maintain a healthy lifestyle and to understand and access healthcare when required. (www.americashealthrankings.org/2008/graduation.html)
Violent Crime	The number of murders, rapes, robberies and aggravated assaults per 100,000 population. It reflects an aspect of overall lifestyle within a state and its associated health risks. (www.americashealthrankings.org/2008/crime.html)
Occupational Fatalities	Number of fatalities from occupational injuries per 100,000 workers. This measure reflects job safety as part of public health. (www.americashealthrankings.org/2008/occupational.html)
Infectious Disease	Number of AIDS, tuberculosis and hepatitis (A and B) cases reported to the Centers for Disease Control and Prevention per 100,000 population. This is an indication of the toll that infectious disease is placing on the population. (www.americashealthrankings.org/2008/disease.html)
Children in Poverty	The percentage of persons under age 18 who live in households at or below the poverty threshold. Poverty is an indication of the lack of access to healthcare by this vulnerable population. (www.americashealthrankings.org/2008/poverty.html)
Air Pollution	The average exposure of the general public to particulate matter of 2.5 microns or less in size (PM2.5). Health studies have shown a significant association between exposure to fine particles and premature death from heart or lung disease. Fine particles can aggravate heart and lung diseases and have been linked to effects such as cardiovascular symptoms; cardiac arrhythmias; heart attacks; respiratory symptoms; asthma attacks and bronchitis. (www.americashealthrankings.org/2008/air.html)
Public Health & Policies	
Lack of Health Insurance	Percentage of the population that does not have health insurance privately, through their employer or the government. This is an indicator of the ability to access care as needed, especially preventive care. (www.americashealthrankings.org/2008/insurance.html)
Public Health Funding	State funding dedicated to public health as well as federal funding directed to states by the Centers for Disease Control and Prevention and the Health Resources and Services Administration, expressed on a per capita basis. This represents the annual investment being made in public health programs to monitor and improve population health. (www.americashealthrankings.org/2008/funding.html)

APPENDIX 6 (continued)
LEXICON of *America's Health Rankings, 2008* HEALTH DETERMINANTS & OUTCOMES

HEALTH DETERMINANTS (continued)	DESCRIPTION
Public Health & Policies	
Immunization Coverage	Percentage of children ages 19 to 35 months who have received four of more doses of DTP, three or more doses of polio vaccine, one or more doses of any measles-containing vaccine, three or more doses of HiB, and three or more doses of HepB vaccine. (www.americashealthrankings.org/2008/immunization.html)
Clinical Care	
Adequacy of Prenatal Care	Percentage of pregnant women receiving adequate prenatal care, as defined by Kotelchuck's Adequacy of Prenatal Care Utilization (APNCU) Index. This measures how well women are receiving the care they require for a healthy pregnancy and development of the fetus. (www.americashealthrankings.org/2008/prenatal.html)
Primary Care Physicians	Number or primary care physicians (including general practice, family practice, OB-GYN, pediatrics and internal medicine) per 100,000 population. This measure reflects the availability of physicians to assist the population with preventive and regular care. (www.americashealthrankings.org/2008/pcp.html)
Preventable Hospitalizations	Discharge rate among the Medicare population for diagnoses that are amenable to non-hospital based care. This reflects how well a population uses the various delivery sites for necessary care. (www.americashealthrankings.org/2008/hospitalizations.html)

HEALTH OUTCOMES	DESCRIPTION
Poor Mental Health days	Number of days in the previous 30 days when a person indicates their activities are limited due to mental health difficulties. This is a general indication of the population's ability to function on a day-to-day basis. (www.americashealthrankings.org/2008/mental.html)
Poor Physical Health Days	Number of days in the previous 30 days when a person indicates their activities are limited due to physical health difficulties. This is a general indication of the population's ability to function on a day-to-day basis. (www.americashealthrankings.org/2008/physical.html)
Geographic Disparity	The variation among the overall mortality rates among the counties within a state. Equality among counties would be expressed by low variation. This measure indicates how equal the outcomes are across a state. www.americashealthrankings.org/2008/geographic.html)
Infant Mortality	Number of infant deaths (before age 1) per 1,000 live births. This is an indication of the prenatal care, access and birth process for both child and mother. (www.americashealthrankings.org/2008/mental.html)
Cardiovascular Deaths	Number of deaths due to all cardiovascular diseases, including heart disease and strokes, per 100,000 population. This is an indication of the toll that these types of diseases place on the population. (www.americashealthrankings.org/2008/cvd/html)
Cancer Deaths	Number of deaths due to all causes of cancer per 100,000 population. This is an indication of the toll cancer places on the population. (www.americashealthrankings.org/2008/cancer.html)
Premature Death	Number of years of potential life lost prior to age 75 per 100,000 population. This is an indication of the number of useful years of life that are not available to a population due to early death. (www.americashealthrankings.org/2008/ypll.html)

Source: United Health Foundation: America's Health Rankings. Available at www.americashealthrankings.org/2008

APPENDIX 7
A COMPARISON of HAWAI'I and MISSISSIPPI HEALTH DETERMINANTS & HEALTH OUTCOMES: America's Health Rankings, 2008

	HAWAII	2008	MISSISSIPPI	2008
HEALTH DETERMINANTS	Value	Rank	Value	Rank
Personal Behaviors				
Prevalence of Smoking (Percent of Population)	17.0	8	23.9	44
Prevalence of Binge Drinking (Percent of Population)	18.1	44	10.3	4
Prevalence of Obesity (Percent of Population)	21.7	2	32.6	50
Community & Environment				
High School Graduation (Percent of incoming 9th graders)	75.1	31	63.3	47
Violent Crime (Offense per 100,000 population)	273	12	291	18
Occupational Fatalities (Deaths per 100,000 workers)	5.5	22	11.1	46
Infectious Disease (Cases per 100,000 population)	15.6	30	18.2	35
Children in Poverty (Percent of persons under age 18)	11.6	5	32.8	50
Air Pollution (Micrograms of fine particles per cubic meter)	4.9	2	13.2	29
Public & Health Policies				
Lack of Health Insurance (Percent without health insurance)	8.2	2	19.8	46
Public Health Funding (Dollars per person)	$198	1	$61	31
Immunization Coverage (Percent of children ages 19 to 35 months)	87.8	4	78.7	34
Clinical Care				
Adequacy of Prenatal Care (Percent of pregnant women)	63.7	—	73.6	—
Primary Care Physicians (Number per 100,000 population)	146.9	7	81.5	48
Preventable Hospitalizations (Number per 1,000 Medicare enrollees)	32.2	1	109.8	47
ALL HEALTH DETERMINANTS	16.0	2	-10.5	49
	HAWAII	2008	MISSISSIPPI	2008
HEALTH OUTCOMES	Value	Rank	Value	Rank
Poor Mental Health Days (Days in previous 30 days)	2.8	7	4.0	49
Poor Physical Health Days (Days in previous 30 days)	2.9	4	4.0	44
Geographic Disparity (Relative standard deviation)	8.8	13	13	36
Infant Mortality (Deaths per 1,000 live births)	6.1	17	10.2	49
Cardiovascular Deaths (Deaths per 100,000 population)	241.1	2	387.0	50
Cancer Deaths (Deaths per 100,000 population)	159.0	1	215.2	46
Premature Death (Years lost per 100,000 population)	6,255	12	11,308	49
ALL HEALTH OUTCOMES	5.5	4	-4.5	50
	Value	Rank	Value	Rank
OVERALL	21.6	2	-15.0	49

Adapted from: United Health Foundation: America's Health Rankings, 2008. Available at: www.americashealthrankings.org/2008

APPENDIX 8
STATE SCORECARD ON HEALTH SYSTEM PERFORMANCE: The Commonwealth Fund

ACCESS	Year	All States Median	Range of State Performance (Bottom-Top)	Top State
1. Adults under age 65 insured	2004-2005	81.5	69.6 – 89.0	MN
2. Children insured	2004-2005	91.1	79.8 – 94.9	VT
3. Adults visited a doctor in past two years	2000	83.4	73.9 – 91.5	DC
4. Adults without a time when they needed to see a doctor but could not because of cost	2004	87.2	80.1 – 96.6	HI
QUALITY				
5. Adults age 50 and older received recommended screening and preventive care	2004	39.7	32.6 – 50.1	MN
6. Adult diabetics received recommended preventive care	2004	42.4	28.7 – 65.4	HI
7. Children ages 19-35 months received all recommended doses of five key vaccines	2005	81.6	66.7 – 93.5	MA
8. Children with both medical and dental preventive care visits	2003	59.2	45.7 – 74.9	MA
9. Children with emotional, behavioral, or developmental problems received mental health care	2003	61.9	43.4 – 77.2	WY
10. Hospitalized patients received recommended care for acute myocardial infarction, congestive heart failure, and pneumonia	2004	83.4	79.0 – 88.4	RI
11. Surgical patients received appropriate timing of antibiotics to prevent infections	2004-2005	69.5	50.0 – 90.0	CT
12. Adults with a usual source of care	2004	81.1	66.3 – 89.4	DE
13. Children with a medical home	2003	47.6	33.8 – 61.0	NH
14. Heart failure patients given written instructions at discharge	2004-2005	49	14 – 67	NJ
15. Medicare patients whose health care provider always listens, explains, shows respect, and spends enough time with them	2003	68.7	63.1 – 74.9	VT
16. Medicare patients giving best rating for health care received	2003	70.2	61.2 – 74.4	MT
17. High-risk nursing home residents with pressure sores	2004	13.2	19.3 – 7.6	ND
18. Nursing home residents who were physically restrained	2004	6.2	15.9 – 1.9	NE
AVOIDABLE USE of HOSPITASLS & COSTS of CARE				
19. Hospital admissions for pediatric asthma per 100,000 children	2002	176.7	314.2 – 54.9	VT
20. Asthmatics with an emergency room or urgent care visit	2001-2004	15.5	29.4 – 9.1	IA
21. Medicare hospital admissions for ambulatory care sensitive conditions per 100,000 beneficiaries	2003	7,278	11,537 – 4,069	HI
22. Medicare 30-day hospital readmission rates	2003	17.6	23.8 – 13.2	VT
23. Long-stay nursing home residents with a hospital admission	2000	16.1	24.9 – 8.3	UT
24. Nursing home residents with a hospital readmission within Three months	2000	11.7	17.5 – 6.7	OR
25. Home health patients with a hospital admission	2004	26.9	46.4 – 18.3	UT
26. Total single premium per enrolled employee at private-sector establishments that offer health insurance	2004	$3,706	$4,379 – 3,034	UT
27. Total Medicare (Parts A & B) reimbursement per enrollee	2003	$6,070	$8,076 – 4,530	HI

APPENDIX 8 (continued)
STATE SCORECARD ON HEALTH SYSTEM PERFORMANCE: The Commonwealth Fund

ACCESS	Year	All States Median	Range of State Performance (Bottom-Top)	Top State
28. Mortality amenable to health care, deaths per 100,000 population	2002	96.9	160.0 – 70.2	MN
29. Infant mortality, deaths per 1,000 live births	2002	7.1	11.0 – 4.3	ME
30. Breast cancer deaths per 100,000 female population	2002	25.3	34.1 – 16.2	HI
31. Colorectal cancer deaths per 100,000 population	2002	20.0	24.6 – 15.3	UT
32. Adults under age 65 limited in any activities because of physical, mental or emotional problems	2004	15.3	22.8 – 10.8	DC

Source: Commonwealth Fund State Scorecard on Health System Performance, 2007. Available at:
http://commonwealthfund.org

APPENDIX 9   **PUBLISHED ARTICLES FROM THE MEDICAL LITERATURE SUPPORTING THE METHODOLOGY AND DATA ANALYSIS UTILIZED in THIS TREATISE**

Litaker, D., 2003. Managed care penetration, insurance status, and access to health care. *Medical Care*, 41(9), pp.1086-1095.
(Available Online at: http://www.jstor.org/pss/3767600)

Qureshi, M., 2000. Differences in breast cancer screening rates: an issue of ethnicity or socioeconomics? *Journal of Women's Health & Gender-Based Medicine*, 9(9), pp. 1025-1032.
(Available Online at:
http://www.liebertonline.com/doi/abs/10.1089/15246090050200060)

* Sox, C., 1998. Insurance or a regular physician: which is the most powerful predictor of health care? *American Journal of Public Health,* 88 (3), 364-370.
(Available Online at:
http://www.ncbi.nlm.nih.gov/pmc/articles/PMC1508345/)

*This National Library of Medicine link provides the entire article, which is particularly relevant to the statistical methodology utilized in this treatise.

APPENDIX 10
OVERVIEW: BRFSS 2007

1. BACKGROUND

The Behavioral Risk Factor Surveillance System (BRFSS) is a collaborative project of the Centers for Disease Control and Prevention (CDC) and U.S. states and territories. The BRFSS, administered and supported by CDC's Behavioral Surveillance Branch, is an ongoing data collection program designed to measure behavioral risk factors in the adult population (18 years of age or older) living in households. The BRFSS was initiated in 1984, with 15 states collecting surveillance data on risk behaviors through monthly telephone interviews. Over time, the number of states participating in the survey increased, so that by 2001, 50 states, the District of Columbia, Puerto Rico, Guam, and the Virgin Islands were participating in the BRFSS. In this document, the term *state* is used to refer to all areas participating in the surveillance system, including the District of Columbia, Guam, the U.S. Virgin Islands, and the Commonwealth of Puerto Rico.

The objective of the BRFSS is to collect uniform, state-specific data on preventive health practices and risk behaviors that are linked to chronic diseases, injuries, and preventable infectious diseases in the adult population. Factors assessed by the BRFSS include tobacco use, health care coverage, HIV/AIDS knowledge and prevention, physical activity, and fruit and vegetable consumption. Data are collected from a random sample of adults (one per household) through a telephone survey.

BRFSS field operations are managed by state health departments, who follow guidelines provided by the CDC. These health departments participate in developing the survey instrument and conduct the interviews either in-house or through use of contractors. The data are transmitted to the CDC's National Center for Chronic Disease Prevention and Health Promotion's Behavioral Surveillance Branch for editing, processing, weighting, and analysis. An edited and weighted data file is provided to each participating health department for each year of data collection, and summary reports of state-specific data are prepared by CDC. Health departments use the data for a variety of purposes, including identifying demographic variations in health-related behaviors, targeting services, addressing emergent and critical health issues, proposing legislation for health initiatives, and measuring progress toward state and national health objectives (1). The health characteristics estimated from the BRFSS pertain to the adult population, aged 18 years and older, who live in households. In 2007 additional questions were included as optional modules to provide a measure for one health characteristic of the non-adult population aged 17 years and less. (These were for childhood asthma prevalence.) As noted above, respondents are identified through telephone-based methods. Although overall, approximately 95 percent of U.S. households have telephones, coverage ranges from 87 to 98 percent across states and varies for subgroups as well. For example, people living in the South, minorities, and those in lower socioeconomic groups typically have lower telephone coverage. No direct method of compensating for non-telephone coverage is employed by the BRFSS; however, post-stratification weights are used, which may partially correct for any bias caused by non-telephone coverage. These weights adjust for differences in probability of selection and nonresponse, as well as noncoverage, and must be used for deriving representative population-based estimates of risk behavior prevalence.

2. DESIGN OF THE BRFSS

A. The BRFSS Questionnaire

The questionnaire has three parts: 1) the core component; 2) optional modules; and 3) state-added questions.

Core component. The *core* is a standard set of questions asked by all states. It includes queries about current health-related perceptions, conditions, and behaviors (e.g., health status, health insurance, diabetes, tobacco use, disability, and HIV/AIDS risks), as well as demographic questions.

Optional CDC modules. These are sets of questions on specific topics (e.g., cardiovascular disease, arthritis, women's health) that states elect to use on their questionnaires. In 2007, 19 optional modules were supported by CDC. The module questions are generally submitted by CDC programs and have been selected for inclusion in the editing and evaluation process by CDC. For more information, see *2007 BRFSS Modules Used By States*, http://apps.nccd.cdc.gov/BRFSSModules/ModByState.asp?Yr=2007

State-added questions. These are questions developed or acquired by participating states and added to their questionnaires. State-added questions are not edited or evaluated by CDC. Each year, the states and CDC agree on the content of the core component and optional modules. Many questions are taken from established national surveys, such as the National Health Interview Survey or the National Health and Nutrition Examination Survey. This practice allows the BRFSS to take advantage of questions that may have been tested and allows states to compare their data with those from other surveys. Any new questions proposed as additions to the BRFSS must go through cognitive testing and field testing prior to their inclusion on the survey. BRFSS guidelines specify that all states ask the core component questions without modification; they may choose to add any, all, or none of the optional modules and may add questions of their choosing at the end of the questionnaire.

Although CDC supported 26 modules in 2007, it is not feasible for a state to use them all. States are selective about which modules and state-specific questions they add, to ensure the questionnaire is kept at a reasonable length (though there is wide variation across states in the total number of questions for a given year, ranging from 0 to approximately 200, in Massachusetts). New questionnaires are implemented in January, and usually remain unchanged throughout the year. However, the flexibility of state-added questions does permit additions, changes, and deletions at any time during the year. The 2007 core and module questionnaire is available at http://apps.nccd.cdc.gov/BRFSSModules/ModByState.asp?Yr=2007

Annual Questionnaire Development

Before the beginning of the calendar year, CDC provides states with the text of the core component and the optional modules that will be supported for the coming year. States select their optional modules and choose any state-added questions. Each state then constructs its questionnaire. The order of the questioning is always the same: the core component is asked first, optional modules are asked next, and state-added questions last. This ordering ensures comparability across states and follows CDC guidelines. Generally, the only changes allowed are limited insertions of state-added questions on topics related to core questions. Such exceptions are to be agreed upon in consultation with CDC. However, despite this flexibility, not all states have adhered to the guidelines. Known deviations from the guidelines are noted in the Comparability of Data section of this document. Once the content (core, modules, and state-added questions) of the questionnaire is determined by a state, a hard-copy or electronic version of the instrument is constructed and sent to CDC. For states with Computer-Assisted Telephone Interview (CATI) systems, this document is used for CATI programming and general reference. The questionnaire is used without changes for one calendar year. The questionnaire is available at http://www.cdc.gov/brfss/questionnaires/questionnaires.htm. If a significant portion of the state population does not speak English, states have the option of translating the questionnaire into other languages. At the present time, CDC provides only a Spanish version of the core questionnaire and optional modules.

B. Sample description

In a telephone survey, such as the BRFSS, a sample record is one telephone number in the list of all telephone numbers selected for dialing. In order to meet the BRFSS standard for the participating states' sample designs, sample records must be justifiable as a probability sample of all households with telephones in the state. All participating areas met this criterion in 2007. Fifty-one projects used a disproportionate stratified sample (DSS) design. Guam, Puerto Rico and the U.S. Virgin Islands used a simple random sample design.

In the type of DSS design most commonly used in the BRFSS, telephone numbers are divided into two groups, or strata, which are sampled separately. The high-density and medium-density strata contain telephone numbers that are expected to belong mostly to households. Whether a telephone number goes into the high-density or medium-density stratum is determined by the number of listed household numbers in its hundred block. A hundred block is a set of one hundred telephone numbers with the same area code, prefix, and first two digits of the suffix and all possible combinations of the last two digits. Numbers that come from hundred blocks with one or more listed household numbers ("1+ blocks," or "banks") are put in the either the high-density stratum ("listed 1+ blocks") or medium-density stratum ("unlisted 1 + blocks"). The two strata are sampled to obtain a probability sample of all households with telephones.

In most cases, each state constitutes a single stratum. However, in order to provide adequate sample sizes for smaller geographically defined populations of interest, some states sample disproportionately from strata defined to correspond to sub-state regions. In 2007, the 42 states with disproportionately sampled geographic strata are Alabama, Alaska, Arizona, California, Connecticut, Delaware, Florida, Georgia, Hawaii, Idaho, Indiana, Iowa, Kentucky, Louisiana, Maine, Maryland, Massachusetts, Michigan, Mississippi, Missouri, Montana, Nebraska, Nevada,

New Hampshire, New Jersey, New Mexico, North Carolina, North Dakota, Ohio, Oklahoma, Pennsylvania, Puerto Rico, Rhode Island, South Carolina, South Dakota, Tennessee, Texas, Utah, Virginia, Virgin Islands, Washington, and Wisconsin.

Data for a state may be collected directly by the state health department or through a contractor. In 2007, 12 state health departments collected their data in-house; 42 contracted data collection to university survey research centers or commercial firms.

In 2007, the Behavioral Surveillance Branch provided samples purchased from Genesys (Marketing Group Systems) to all 54 states or territories.

3. DATA COLLECTION

Interviewing Procedures

In 2007, 53 states used computer-assisted telephone interviewing (CATI). CDC supports CATI programming using the Ci3 CATI software package. This support includes programming the core and module questions for data collectors, providing questionnaire scripting of state-added questions for states requiring such assistance, and contracting with a Ci3 consultant who is available to assist states. Following guidelines provided by CDC, state health personnel or contractors conduct interviews. The core portion of the questionnaire lasts an average of 10 minutes. Interview time for modules and state-added questions is dependent upon the number of questions used, but generally extend the interview period by an additional 5 to 10 minutes. nterviewer retention is very high among states that conduct the survey in-house. The state coordinator or interviewer supervisor usually conducts the training using materials developed by CDC. These materials cover seven basic areas: overview of the BRFSS, role descriptions for staff involved in the interviewing process, the questionnaire, sampling, codes and dispositions (three-digit codes indicating the outcome of each call attempts), survey follow-up, and practice sessions. Contractors typically use interviewers who have experience conducting telephone surveys, but these interviewers are given additional training on the BRFSS questionnaire and procedures before they are approved to work on BRFSS. Further specifics on interviewer training and procedures are available, *http://www.cdc.gov/brfss/training.htm*.

CDC expects interviewer performance to be monitored. In 2007, all BRFSS surveillance sites had the capability to monitor their interviewers. The system used for monitoring interviewers varied from listening to the interviewer only at an on-site location to listening to both the interviewer and respondent at a remote location. Verification call-backs were also used by some states in lieu of direct monitoring. Contractors typically conducted systematic monitoring by monitoring each interviewer a certain amount of time each month. All states had the capability to tabulate disposition code frequencies by interviewer. These data were the primary means for quantifying interviewer performance. All states were required to do verification callbacks for a sample of completed interviews as part of their quality control practices.

Telephone interviewing was conducted during each calendar month, and calls were made seven days per week, during both daytime and evening hours. Standard procedures were followed for rotation of calls over days of the week and time of day. BRFSS procedural rules are described in the *BRFSS User's Guide,* http://www.cdc.gov/brfss/pubrfdat.htm#users .

Detailed information on interview response rates and item nonresponse rates are discussed in the *2007 Summary Data Quality Report.*

4. DATA PROCESSING

A. Preparing for data collection and data processing

Data processing is an integral part of any survey. Because data are collected and sent to CDC during each month of the year, there are routine data processing tasks that need attention on an ongoing basis throughout the year. In addition, there are tasks that need to be conducted at different points in the annual BRFSS cycle. The preparation for the survey involves a number of steps that take place once the new questionnaire is finalized. This includes developing the edit specifications, programming portions of the Ci3 CATI software, programming the PC-EDITS software, and producing telephone sample estimates for states that require them and ordering the sample from the contract vendor. A Ci3-CATI data entry module for each state that uses this software is produced. Skip patterns, together with some consistency edits, and response-code range checks are incorporated into the CATI system. These edits and skip patterns serve to reduce interviewer, data entry, and skip errors. Data conversion tables are then developed. These tables are used for reading the survey data from the entry module, calling information from the sample tracking module, and combining information into the final format specified for the data year. CDC also creates and distributes a Windows-based editing program that can perform data validations on properly formatted survey results files. This program is used to output lists of errors or warning conditions encountered in the data.

CDC begins to process data for the survey year as soon as states or their contractors begin submitting data to the data management mailbox, and continues processing data throughout the survey year. CDC receives and tracks monthly data submissions from the states. Once data are received from the state, editing programs and cumulative data quality checks are run against the data. Any problems in the file are noted, and a CDC programmer works with the state until the problems are resolved or agreement is reached that no resolution is possible. Response-rate data quality reports are produced and shared with the project officers and state coordinators, who review the reports and discuss any potential problems with the state. Once the entire year of data for a state has been received and validated, several year-end programs are run on the data. These programs perform some additional, limited data cleanup and fixes specific to the state and data year, and produce reports that identify potential analytic problems with the data set. Once these programs have been run, the data are ready for assigning weights and adding new variables.

Not all of the variables that appear on the public use data set are taken directly from the state files. CDC prepares a set of SAS programs that are used for end-of-year data processing. These programs prepare the data for analysis and add weighting and risk factor calculations as variables to the data file. The following variables are examples of results from this procedure, and are created for the user's convenience: _RFSMOK3, _MRACE, _AGEG, _TOTINDA. (For more information, see the Calculated Variables and Risk Factors in Data Files document at

) To create these variables, several variables from the data file are combined. The process of creating these variables varies in complexity; some are based only on combined codes, while others require sorting and combining of selected codes from multiple variables.

Almost every variable derived from the BRFSS interview has a code category labeled "refused" and generally given a value of "9," "99," or "999" value. Typically, the category consists of non-interviews (a "non-interview" response results when an interview is terminated prior to this question and an interviewer codes the remaining responses as "refused") and persons for whom the question was not applicable because of a previous response or a personal characteristic (e.g., age). However, this code may capture some questions that were supposed to be answered, but for some reason were not, and appeared as a blank or other symbol. The combination of these types of responses into a single code requires vigilance on the part of data file users who wish to separate respondents who were skipped out of a question from those who were asked, but whose answer was unknown or who refused to answer a particular question.

B. Weighting the data

When data are used without weights, each record counts the same as any other record. Implicit in such use are the assumptions that each record has an equal probability of being selected and that noncoverage and nonresponse are equal among all segments of the population. When deviations from these assumptions are large enough to affect the results obtained from a data set, then weighting each record appropriately can help to adjust for assumption violations. An additional, but conceptually unrelated, reason for weighting is to make the total number of cases equal to some desired number which, for state BRFSS data, is the number of people in the state who are age 18 and older. In the BRFSS, such poststratification serves as a blanket adjustment for noncoverage and nonresponse and forces the total number of cases to equal population estimates for each geographic region, which for the BRFSS is usually a state.

Following is a general formula that reflects all the factors taken into account in weighting the 2007 BRFSS data. Where a factor does not apply its value is set to one for calculation.

$$\text{FINALWT} = \text{STRWT} \times \text{1 OVER NPH} \times \text{NAD} \times \text{POSTSTRAT}$$

FINALWT is the final weight assigned to each respondent.

STRWT accounts for differences in the basic probability of selection among strata (subsets of area code/prefix combinations). It is the inverse of the sampling fraction of each stratum. There is seldom a complete correspondence between strata, which are defined by subsets of area code/prefix combinations, and regions, which are defined by the boundaries of government entities.

1/NPH is the inverse of the number of residential telephone numbers in the respondent's household.

NAD is the number of adults in the respondent's household.

POSTSTRAT is the number of people in an age-by-sex or age-by-race/ethnicity-by-sex category in the population of a region or a state divided by the sum of the preceding weights for the respondents in the same age-by-sex or age-by-race/ethnicity-by-sex category. It adjusts for noncoverage and nonresponse and forces the sum of the weighted frequencies to equal population estimates for the region or state.

CHILDWT = STRWT × 1 OVER NPH × CHILDREN × POSTCH

CHILDWT is the final weight assigned to each child.

STRWT accounts for differences in the basic probability of selection among strata (subsets of area code/prefix combinations). It is the inverse of the sampling fraction of each stratum. There is almost never a complete correspondence between strata, which are defined by subsets of area code/prefix combinations, and regions, which are defined by the boundaries of government entities.

1/NPH is the inverse of the number of residential telephone numbers in the respondent's household.

CHILDREN is the number of children (less than 18 years of age) in the respondent's household.

POSTCH is the number of children in an age-by-gender or age-by-race-by-gender category in the population of a region or a state divided by the sum of the preceding weights for the children in that same age-by-gender or age-by-race-by-gender category. It adjusts for non-coverage and non-response.

HOUSEWT = STRWT × 1 OVER NPH × POSTHH

HOUSEWT is the weight assigned to each household.

STRWT accounts for differences in the basic probability of selection among strata (subsets of area code/prefix combinations). It is the inverse of the sampling fraction of each stratum. There is almost never a complete correspondence between strata, which are defined by subsets of area code/prefix combinations, and regions, which are defined by the boundaries of government entities.

1/NPH is the inverse of the number of residential telephone numbers in the household.

POSTHH is the number of households in the population of a region or a state divided by the sum of the products of the preceding weights for the households in that same category. It adjusts for non-coverage and non-response.

ITSADJWT = ITSCF2 × ITSPOST

ITSADJWT is the weight adjustment for non-telephone households or interruption in telephone service for 1 week or more during the past 12 months.

An estimate of the total number of adults in households with telephones and without telephones is obtained from the latest CPS data. The estimate of the total number of adults in households with telephone service interruptions is combined with the estimate of adults in non-telephone households. This total is used to determine a ratio to adjust the base weights of respondents with telephone service interruptions. The estimate of the total number of adults in households with no telephone service interruptions is used to determine a ratio to adjust the base weights of respondents with no telephone service interruptions. The data is then post-stratified to the BRFSS population totals.

ITSCF2 is the interruption in telephone service correction factor (adjusted _WT2) using the variable TELSERV (indication of interruption in telephone service) response and the number of adults in households without telephones.

ITSPOST is the number of households in the population of a region or a state divided by the sum of the products of the preceding weights for the households in that same category. It adjusts for non-coverage and non-response.

REFERENCES

1. Remington PL, Smith MY, Williamson DF, Anda RF, Gentry EM, Hogelin GC. Design, characteristics, and usefulness of state-based behavioral risk factor surveillance: 1981–87. Public Health Reports. 1988; 103(4): 366–375.

2. Bureau of the Census. Phoneless in America. Statistical Brief 94–16. U. S. Department of Commerce, Bureau of the Census. July 1994.